Manifesting Your Best Future Self

Manifesting Your Best Future Self

Developing Health, Happiness, and Success

DR PETER GRUENEWALD, MD

Copyright © 2020 Dr Peter Gruenewald, MD
All rights reserved.

ISBN: 979-8-6791-9047-4

Book and cover design by Madison Lux.
Edited by Hannah Skaggs.

No part of this book may be reproduced, stored, or transmitted by any means—whether auditory, graphic, mechanical, or electronic—without written permission of both publisher and author, except in the case of brief excerpts used in critical articles and reviews. Unauthorized reproduction of any part of this work is illegal and is punishable by law.

The training program provided in this manual is not a substitute for advice, treatment, or counseling from a registered health professional or therapist. A health professional or therapist should be consulted in the case of suspected physical or mental illness. The training is not a substitute for any intervention advised by your healthcare provider or therapist. If in doubt, always consult your healthcare provider or therapist.

Because of the dynamic nature of the Internet, any web addresses or links contained in this book may have changed since publication and may no longer be valid. The views expressed in this work are solely those of the author and do not necessarily reflect the views of the publisher, and the publisher hereby disclaims any responsibility for them.

Contents

What Is Adaptive Resilience?...................1
Exercise 1: Coherence Training 17
The Breath Pacer.............................21
Rescue Breath 31
Case Study: Overcoming Misery 37
Exercise 2: Quick Stress Relief 39
Exercise 3: In-Step Technique................41
Exercise 4: A Courageous Conversation with Myself
           (Positive Self-Talk) 47
Strengthen Your Willpower and Attract Favorable Circumstances..53
Case Study: Living with a Demanding Mother 55
Exercise 5: Mindful Nature Observation 61
Exercise 6: Active Listening 63
Case Study: Preparing for a Difficult Meeting 69
Exercise 7: Transforming Difficult Relationships 71
Case Study: Frustration of a Teenager 77
Summary and Conclusion.....................................81
About the Author 83
References 87

What Is Adaptive Resilience?

Adaptive resilience is about transforming raw emotions into higher feelings, building resilience, improving and protecting health, and enhancing performance and productivity.

TED speaker, psychologist, former management consultant, and teacher Angela Lee Duckworth wanted to know what makes people successful in this day and age. She studied people in various industries, from the military to students in spelling contests to teachers working in rough neighborhoods to executives in private companies. In all these different contexts, one trait emerged as a significant predictor of success. Duckworth said, "It wasn't social intelligence, it wasn't good looks, physical health, and it wasn't IQ. It was grit. Grit is passion and perseverance for very long-term goals. Grit is having stamina. Grit is sticking with your future day in, day out, not just for the week, not just for the month, but for years, and working really hard to make that future a reality. Grit is living life like it's a marathon, not a sprint."[1]

No one is free from problems in life. Even if you can't think of major obstacles, you're bound to be challenged by the changes in your life, especially fast changes. We know grit is an important factor to succeed through change and challenges, and we see that it can be built by developing resilience skills and a "growth mindset."[2]

Now, some of you may think, "But I don't want to persevere to reach long-term goals. It's too hard. I prefer to live life in the moment and take things as they happen." Adaptive resilience is not just about being able to bounce back or press on despite obstacles, but the ability to prevent pitfalls and embrace problems in a flexible way, emerging in an even stronger homeodynamic position.

Hungarian psychologist Mihaly Csíkszentmihályi[3] found that "flow states" (i.e., moments of being "in the zone") are key to a person's happiness.[4] With adaptive resilience, you'll find that life feels like neither a marathon nor a sprint, but a dance in which you are in the zone.

STRESS, HEALTH, AND PERFORMANCE

Most of us wish to be happy, fulfilled, and successful. Psychological studies have investigated character traits of those who, despite facing major challenges in life, consider themselves as having achieved these goals. The studies show that people are most resilient in the face of trouble if they can shift from the negative emotions experienced at times of crisis—such as anger, frustration, sadness, despair, and guilt—toward positive feelings such as forgiveness, compassion, self-compassion, appreciation, and gratitude.[5, 6]

Emotional intelligence, one of the most important skills for success in life, is the ability to recognize and regulate our own emotional responses, and likewise recognize and help regulate the emotions of others. Emotional intelligence can be learned. We can become (more) aware of our emotions and feelings, and more openly acknowledge them. We can learn to shift intentionally from negative to positive feelings, thus developing core skills of resilience and becoming better able to master life's adversities.[7]

Very few of us live in constant bliss, happiness, and harmony; frequent and continual challenges seem to be intrinsic to our lives. At work and at home, we experience all kinds of pressures: financial and professional pressures, strain in our relationships and in connection with childcare and parenting, the stress of moving to a new house or dealing with grief, and other forms of enforced change and crisis such as loss of status or possessions.

And we expect to and are expected to cope, to look happy, but also to continue being good or excellent in everything we do.

Amid all these pressures, our inner voice may ask us whether we're really in command of our own responses, whether we're leading the life we really want to, and whether we can guide our own life and support others, both at home and at work, in the ways we desire.

Sometimes we succeed in silencing this voice, perhaps by drowning it out with shopping, alcohol, comfort eating, or extreme sports, or by throwing ourselves into frantic work. But ultimately, we can't escape these questions forever. They're implicit in who we are or who we want to be.

Positive and motivational psychology focus on a very important and also very useful question: how can people become more self-determined (autonomy), happier, and more successful? But also, how can they simply become more content with their life as it is now?

Adaptive resilience sets out to give you simple, proven tools and techniques. These are easy to practice, and when used for just a few minutes each day, they have led to big changes for many people, helping them live happier, healthier, and more successful lives.[8]

All the techniques introduced here are based on scientific research in neurophysiology, chronobiology, neuropsychology, mindfulness, and positive and motivational psychology. All have been carefully researched and shown to be safe and effective.

We start with understanding the power of emotions to affect health, happiness, and success. These include both the emotions we know about and the ones we may be unaware of that subconsciously and profoundly affect our judgment, decision-making, and behavior.

Stress and extreme emotions have powerful repercussions for your health. Although short-term stress has a strong positive impact on performance and can also make us more resilient, exposure to high levels of pressure over long time periods without proper recovery undermines health, performance, and happiness. Extreme emotions, particularly those we aren't fully aware of, can have a strong negative influence on our health and performance.[9]

However, emotions such as anxiety, fear, grief, anger, frustration, disappointment, and despair can also have a beneficial effect in our lives because they can make us aware of risks and problems and also spark the will for deep change. But being unaware of them, not acknowledging or accepting them, or experiencing them constantly over longer periods of time and with high intensity will undermine our health and reduce our capacity for good judgment, decision-making, and meaningful and effective action.

The exercises and techniques described here can not only help you become more aware of how you feel and what you want, but also reduce the impact of extreme emotions that undermine your health and performance. At the same time, the training can help you transform these emotions into greater calm, love, passion, compassion and self-compassion, forgiveness, and confidence, feelings that are key to improving health, performance, resilience, and ultimately happiness and success.[10]

Applying these exercises and techniques in your daily work and private life will allow you to move from negative to positive emotional states at will, even under pressure and in crisis. Most people can learn to do this without much effort, even late in life and even if they had difficult beginnings in childhood.

BEING RESILIENT

Having adaptive resilience is having a healthy and reliable physiological, mental, and emotional regulatory system that allows you to effectively manage change, maximize your potentials, be authentic, do things you enjoy, and be productive without feeling hurried or overstressed. On the other hand, a lack of adaptive resilience may result in excessive strain and tension, or numbness and disengagement from life, depression, and anxiety, as well as missed opportunities for growth. But virtually anyone can learn how to become resilient through simple yet consistent practical exercises.

ABOUT OUR APPROACH

This approach to adaptive resilience combines insights and evidence from chronobiology (the study of biological rhythms and their adaptation to the environment), physiology, positive psychology, existential psychology and neuropsychology, social science, and mindfulness to provide a holistic method for resilience. Human beings are dynamic and complex, and we've found evidence of the multidirectional relationship between body, mind, and spirit as well as practical skills that help you connect these components effectively. We therefore take a bio-psycho-social-spiritual approach to resilience, building you up from the top down (engaging the mind in important questions), as well as from the bottom up (changing your physiology, like heart rate variability).

The adaptive resilience approach offers simple exercises as practical tools and techniques created to help you develop resilience, improve well-being and health, and deal effectively with pressure.

I will define adaptive resilience, summarize the research and case studies that show how we develop resilience, discuss what these factors look like in the brain and body, and provide practical exercises you can do to develop these resilience skills. You'll learn ways to train yourself to achieve more of those flow states Csíkszentmihályi describes, through exercises that boost both your sympathetic and parasympathetic nervous systems and increase connection and engagement with people and tasks.

You'll also hear about methods to aid release, recovery, and recuperation after strenuous activities.

Afterward, I will cover concepts such as cognitive flexibility, detaching and engaging at will and training the mind to be flexible and wise in doing the right things at the right time.

The practical exercises recommended in this book are all scientifically proven to be effective. Having said that, research speaks for most but not all people, and each person is different. We encourage you to personalize the exercises. Feel free to practice the skills you most resonate with and make them your own. You may also have found yourself practicing some of them already, but we may show you how to do them in a different and more conscious way to help you become more consistent.

WHAT IS ADAPTIVE RESILIENCE?

When we're adaptively resilient, we show flexibility, creativity, and capability to work effectively with others under both everyday stresses and unusually challenging times—even in a crisis. Developing adaptive resilience entails getting to know our bodies and developing skills and habits that enable us to maintain good health, judgment, decision-making, and performance, even under sustained high pressure.

Adaptive resilience is the positive capacity to cope with stress and catastrophe—to bounce back to a state of flexible balance after a disruption. Resilience helps you develop protective factors: resourcefulness and mental toughness. Resilience is also a strong foundation for better emotional and physical health, even when you're exposed to long-term pressure or crisis. With adaptive resilience, you can more readily shift your energy from negative emotions to positive feelings. The shift from negative emotions such as anxiety, fear, anger, and frustration toward acceptance, appreciation, gratitude, and (self-)compassion in the face of adversity is a core element of resilience. It promotes emotional and physical health and keeps you at peak performance and productivity under pressure.[11]

FOUR AREAS OF RESILIENCE

We recognize four areas of resilience, all equally important to our health, happiness, and success in life:

- **Physical resilience** is achieved and maintained through good nutrition, good sleep quality and duration, fitness and stamina,

rhythmic alteration between strain and recovery, and a rhythmic lifestyle. *Supporting AR exercise: Coherence Training, which also benefits all other areas of resilience*
- **Mental resilience** is achieved and maintained through good judgment and decision-making under pressure, belief in yourself, a positive outlook and perspective, sustained focus, a good understanding of causality, and an ability to control the environment. *Supporting AR exercises: In-Step Technique, Courageous Conversation*
- **Emotional resilience** is achieved and maintained through awareness, acknowledgment, and acceptance of emotions; ability to neutralize negative emotions; and ability to control impulses. It depends on developing positive life-, health-, and performance-enhancing feelings (positive emotions) and maintaining a realistic optimism. *Supporting AR exercises: Gratitude exercise, In-Step Technique, Coherence Training*
- **Spiritual resilience** is achieved and maintained by developing and achieving life goals (sense of purpose), values (ethics), autonomy (self-determination), love (empathy), and mastery (competence). *Supporting AR exercises: Courageous Conversation, Coherence Training*

Of course, these four areas are not completely separate from each other, and often rely on each other: a strong sense of purpose with clear life goals and values will affect our emotions, creating passion and enthusiasm for life, which in turn shape our outlook and perspective and have a health-enhancing effect.

Just relying on physical or some mental exercises to develop more resilience may work for a while since it improves stress tolerance, but it may not enhance our emotional intelligence, which, if developed, positively affects our social relationships.

Positive emotions enhance vitality and health. Here are two examples: (1) Realistic optimists live an average of 10 years longer than pessimists[12] and (2) men who have suffered a heart attack are less likely to experience a second heart attack if they return to a home environment where they feel loved and/or appreciated.[13]

In turn, many people experience a serious personal crisis and even a major depression if they have neglected to find their personal sense of purpose, which may have to go beyond purely material values. Or they may fall out with each other if they fail to recognize, accept, and shift their emotions and feelings. Over time, resentment replaces mutual understanding and goodwill. People with long-standing negative emotional experiences, such as depression and anxiety, are much more likely to develop chronic heart disease, such as life-threatening arrhythmia and heart attacks, later in life.[14]

Our approach is based on the neuroscience of cognition, emotion, and behavior and the physical rhythms that both govern and are governed by our bodies' responses to the stresses and challenges of life.

Heart rate variability (chronobiology) is a fundamental key to health and performance. Another key is mindfulness: living in the now, with the capacity to deliberately and actively connect or detach yourself from life's events. We incorporate elements of cognitive behavior therapy that are "problem-focused" and "action-oriented."

Positive psychology, with its emphasis on positive emotions and development of psychological resilience, is another key to happiness and success.

Finally, through motivational psychology, we strive to develop goal-oriented behavior, life purpose, and success.

By practicing and incorporating these psychological and physiological approaches to adaptive resilience, our patients/clients learn how to improve and maintain their emotional and physical health. They recognize, acknowledge, and understand disturbing emotions—and how to let go of them. They develop the skills and habits that support and sustain positive emotions and feelings. They're able to build and sustain healthy and caring personal relationships and effective, mutually rewarding working relationships. And by developing their adaptive resilience, they're able to thrive under pressure, making good judgments and decisions.

When you develop high levels of adaptive resilience in all areas of your life, you experience good outcomes, regardless of how risky the situation appears. You maintain your competence even under stress, and you can recover quickly and completely from trauma. Both your mind and body gain resilience, so you can recover more quickly from illness or injury.

THE SYMPATHETIC NERVOUS SYSTEM

The sympathetic nervous system (SNS) is responsible for mobilizing energy in challenging situations. It gives the physiological foundation for the "fight or flight" response by raising the heart rate and blood pressure, pushes the blood away from the skin and inner organs toward the muscles, and can move us away from lengthy consideration toward fast reflex responses. When sympathetic activity is in overdrive for a long time, this stress can manifest in a number of health problems, such as hypertension, cardiovascular disease, diabetes, etc.

The SNS is particularly active during the light phases of sleep, such as sleep phases 1 and 2 and REM sleep. During REM sleep, we process our daytime experiences through dreaming. This happens even though we may not be aware of it.

When all is going well, the overall activity of the SNS markedly decreases during sleep, then increases during the day. The cycle allows for good daytime performance and undisturbed recovery during sleep.

THE PARASYMPATHETIC NERVOUS SYSTEM

The parasympathetic nervous system (PNS) is responsible for the ability to regenerate and recover during times of rest or relaxation, when digesting, and while asleep. During the day, it also creates the physiological foundation for the "tending and befriending" response, a parasympathetic stress relief response accompanied by increasing levels of oxytocin in the blood and brain. Oxytocin reduces anxiety and increases feelings of trust and bonding.

Physiologically, parasympathetic activity lowers the heart rate and blood pressure, speeds up digestion, centralizes the blood, and helps us access the creative forces of our subconscious mind. Driven to the extreme, however, by high levels of sustained pressure (stress), the PNS may lead to a freeze response (pretend-to-be-dead reflex) during waking, a state of disconnection from life, a sense of numbness and paralysis of will. This happens when the situation becomes so hopeless, there's no way out except to pretend to be dead. This state can result from burnout, trauma, and/or chronic poor sleep.

When we sleep, parasympathetic activity facilitates recovery; it's especially active during deep sleep phases 3 and 4, particularly during the first part of the night.

When all is going well, there is strong parasympathetic activity during sleep, but also some parasympathetic activity during the day, as all activities that involve our full engagement and creativity, such as problem solving, are best supported by balanced and rhythmic sympathetic and parasympathetic activity (autonomic balance).

SUMMARY

The autonomic nervous system (ANS) has two parts with opposite and complementary functions.

- Sympathetic system
    - Engages activation response
    - Mobilizes and alerts
    - Engages "fight or flight" response
    - Speeds up the heart

- Parasympathetic system
    » Engages "freeze or flop" response
    » Relaxes and regenerates
    » Engages "tending and befriending" response
    » Slows the heart down

When the sympathetic nervous system is dominant, we experience negative stress and tension. If SNS dominance is not counterbalanced and goes on too long, it can lead to chronic conditions such as premature aging, arteriosclerosis, hypertension, diabetes, and cancer. A chronic inflammatory process lies under all these conditions, and it's enhanced when we experience negative emotions such as stress, anger, and anxiety over a long period of time.

The parasympathetic nervous system (vagal nerve) is engaged during relaxation, sleep, and digestion. It's responsible for recovery after strain and works opposite the sympathetic nervous system. PNS dominance, often found after trauma or with burnout, may be experienced as ongoing fatigue, daytime sleepiness, emotional withdrawal, lack of drive, and even depression. It can also manifest in the form of a "premature inner retirement," which happens when we move our body into work, but our mind is somewhere else. This is a state of "freeze or flop," or a simple withdrawal into boredom.

The sympathetic and parasympathetic nervous systems need to be in dynamic balance and constant flux. Any permanent fixation of this relationship or age-inappropriate dominance of one system over the other will lead to illness and reduced well-being and performance.

SYMPTOMS OF SYMPATHETIC OR PARASYMPATHETIC DOMINANCE

Stress & Resilience	Sympathetic Dominance	Engagement (Balance)	Parasympathetic Dominance
Physiological	High heart rate High blood pressure High inflammation Irregular heart rate High arousal Insomnia Arrhythmia	Normal heart rate Normal blood pressure Balanced ANS High stamina High resilience	Low heart rate Low blood pressure Low inflammation Low arousal Sleepiness Fatigue
Emotional	Tension Anxiety Fear Anger Shame	Appreciation Gratitude Enthusiasm Empathy Courage	Numbness Disconnection Disassociation Depression
Behavioral	Fight or flight Impulsiveness Risk taking Rigidity Competitiveness	Sustainable peak performance	Freeze or flop Avoidance Inhibition Procrastination
Mental	Poor judgments Poor decisions	Good judgments Good decisions Imagination Inspiration	Indecisiveness Hesitation

THE PHYSIOLOGY OF ENGAGEMENT AND FLOW

We all know what it feels like to be put on the spot unexpectedly; our heart may pound and we may feel butterflies in the stomach, get a dry mouth, breathe shallowly and quickly, or even lose our voice.

Even the most experienced actors describe a feeling of stage fright before they go out on stage. They'll also tell you they need this stage fright to perform well in challenging circumstances, i.e., during a performance. Stage fright is tied to increased physiological stress, a fight or flight response that's alerting and mobilizing; it keeps actors awake and literally on their toes.

But the surprising thing is what happens when the experienced performing artist is out on stage: all stress symptoms are replaced by an excellent performance based on complete identification with the role, the act of performing, and the strong connection with the audience. This is a state of engagement, a third state between strain and recovery.

Measuring the functioning of the autonomic nervous system with heart rate variability assessments shows that the activities of engagement involve cooperation between the sympathetic and parasympathetic nervous systems.

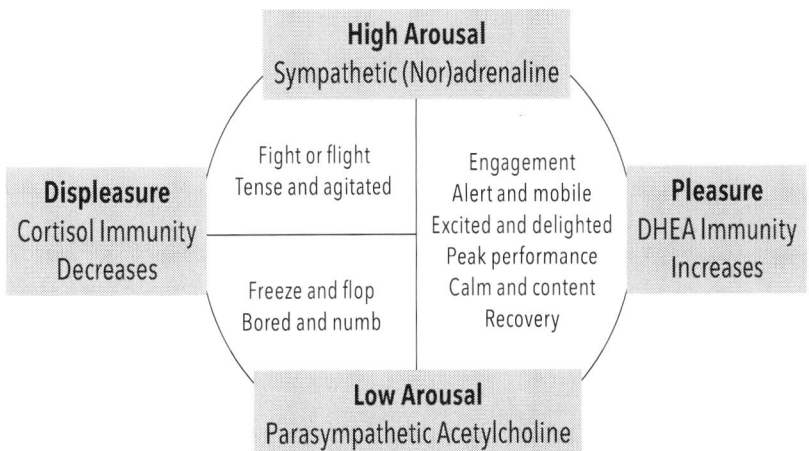

The resulting physiological state of engagement has the following characteristics:

1. Sustainable Peak Performance

People who are in a state of engagement can problem-solve well in challenging circumstances, are creative, make good judgments and decisions under duress, and are highly productive. Despite excellent performance and productivity, people don't tire as quickly in this state as when they're in a state of tension. This is because, during engagement, both parts of the ANS are activated at the same time. The SNS contributes to alertness and mobility, while the PNS supports playfulness, artistry, and recovery. Negative aspects of a fixed, one-sided nervous system dynamic—such as fight or flight, freeze or flop, and social isolation with rigid behavior patterns—are transformed through the positive aspects of alertness and mobility (sympathetic) and the tend and befriend response (parasympathetic).

2. Flow

Positive psychologist Mihály Csíkszentmihályi describes flow as the mental state in which a person performing an activity is fully immersed in a feeling of energized focus, full involvement, and enjoyment in the process of the activity. In essence, flow involves complete absorption in what we're doing, being "in the zone."

According to Csíkszentmihályi, flow is completely focused motivation. It's a single-minded immersion, probably the ultimate experience in harnessing the emotions to sustain peak performance and learning. In flow, the emotions are not just contained and channeled, but positive, energized, and aligned with the task at hand. Feelings experienced while performing a task in flow are spontaneous joy, passion, enthusiasm, and love. Still, the individual is focused only on the activity rather than on the self or their own feelings and emotions.

Csíkszentmihályi identified the following six factors as encompassing an experience of flow:

- Intense and focused concentration on the present moment
- Merging of action and awareness
- Loss of reflective self-consciousness
- Sense of personal control or agency over the situation or activity
- An altered subjective experience of time
- Perception of the activity as intrinsically rewarding and strongly connected with a sense of purpose

In Csíkszentmihályi's description of flow, we see the state of engagement. We've identified the physiological correlate of this flow state in the rhythmic and balanced cooperation between sympathetic and parasympathetic activity.[15]

3. Positive Emotional Attitude and Empathetic Interaction

We see the same physiological effect of simultaneous, rhythmic, and balanced interaction of SNS and PNS activity when focusing on a positive feeling, such as gratitude or self-confidence. We've also found that the physiological state of sympathetic and parasympathetic cooperation occurs when two people interact with empathy.

POSITIVE EMOTIONS

Research into resilience has shown a close link between the capacity to shift from negative to positive emotions and the capacity to stay well and healthy and perform well under pressure.[16]

Positive emotions were found to help resilient people

- Disrupt the experience of stress and recover efficiently from daily stress.

- Construct psychological resources they need to cope successfully with adversity and significant catastrophes.
- Notice positive meanings within the problems they faced (e.g., feel grateful to be alive after a terrorist attack).

Positive emotions can cause a number of health benefits related to

- Balancing the autonomic nervous system.
- Strengthening the immune system.
- Reducing chronic inflammation (preventing cardiovascular disease and reducing cancer risk).
- Recovering faster from physical and emotional trauma, heart attacks, and infections.
- Improving emotional and mental health.

It's important to understand that we're not talking about positivity, but about positive emotions. You may have a positive mindset, but the emotions triggered by your memories may still be negative. The emotions we are the least aware of, so-called subconscious emotions, affect our physiology, health, and performance profoundly.

To overcome this split between thoughts and (subconscious) emotions and to line up our thinking (brain) and feeling (heart), we can use techniques that let us create an effective partnership between the conscious and subconscious mind.

EXERCISE 1:
Coherence Training

BENEFITS

- Trains your bodily systems toward flexibility, rhythm, and balance[17, 18]
- Enhances emotional regulation[19, 20]
- Reduces the negative impact of anger, stress, anxiety, and depression[21, 22, 23, 24, 25]
- Enhances your capacity to stay well and perform well under pressure[26]
- Improves general health, well-being and performance[27]
- Reduces symptoms of post-traumatic stress disorder[28]

INTRODUCTION

The Coherence Exercise helps develop meditative and reflective skills while significantly reducing stress. It also helps develop core values such as calmness and security, caring and appreciation, and strength and confidence, addressing each of these qualities individually. Its symbols and affirmations support the deepening of the particular experiences. This powerful breath meditation reduces the negative impact of stress and extreme emotions. It improves and protects physical and emotional health, well-being, and productivity, even under pressure and in crisis.

The Coherence Exercise combines elements of gratitude, guided breathing, focused relaxation, dynamic visualization, and brainwave entrainment. The latter gives access to fully alert states of extended consciousness and increases the effectiveness of subsequent exercises by allowing us to access our higher self and subconscious mind. Physiologically, the exercise balances our autonomic nervous system and endocrine (hormonal) function and strengthens our immune system.

Coherence Training (CT) is an audio-guided and biofeedback-based form of resonant frequency training. It combines paced breathing, dynamic visualization, and brainwave entrainment at gamma 40 Hz and alpha 10 Hz, which are dominant brain waves during flow and peak performance. Inaudible isochronic tones entrain the rhythm of the brain, while the breath pacer entrains the rhythm of the heart. As a result, the training aligns the nervous systems of the brain, heart, and gut.

CT trains to a physiological state that underlies sustainable peak performance, flow state and engagement, and ability to release, relax, and recover, even under pressure. This can lead to better management of stress and extreme emotions, improved and sustained emotional and physical health, and better performance.

CT facilitates and protects emotional and physical health and productivity even under pressure.

Diaphragmatic breathing at a pace of 5.5 breathing cycles per minute has been shown to align the rhythms of breathing, blood pressure, and heart rate variability. The result of this alignment is a resonance effect that enhances the amplitude of heart rate variability, a sign that the autonomic nervous system is flexible, adaptable, and balanced. This increase in heart rate variability (SDNN) and ANS balance point to physical, emotional, and mental health.

During this paced, slow, and deep breathing process, heart and brain enter a state of coherence, which leads to high amplitude synchronized electric activity of heart and brain, shown in the electrocardiogram

EXERCISE 1: COHERENCE TRAINING

(ECG) as electric activity of heart rate variability peaking in the range of 0.1 Hz. In the electroencephalogram (EEG), it's shown in increased brain activity in the range of Alpha 10 Hz. Mid-alpha-brainwave activity is a sign of focused relaxation, when the focus turns from sensory perceptions toward inner experiences in a relaxed but watchful manner. Similar activities of heart and brain also occur when experiencing positive emotions or during a state of flow or engagement.

The breathing exercise is greatly enhanced by using the dynamic visualization of rhythmically alternating and breath-synchronized attention and focus on body and surroundings (flow of sunlight), while experiencing a positive feeling such as gratitude, appreciation, or love. Gratitude, for example, has been shown to promote profound mental, emotional, and physical health benefits.

Coherence breathing can help you better manage stress and reduce extreme emotions such as tension, anxiety, fear, sadness, and anger. It has also been shown to improve emotional and physical health and productivity and build personal and interpersonal resilience.

This exercise activates and energizes the collaboration between heart, brain, and gut nervous systems, and stirs the rest of the body through resonance and coherence. As a result, you may be able to change old neural pathways in your brain and build new ones, positively transforming the way you think, feel, and act.

Practicing this exercise daily over six weeks may make you feel calmer, more energized, and more optimistic over time, and can help you stay well and perform better under stress. Your focus, concentration, and working memory may improve, along with your personal and professional relationships. You may find that you recover faster from strain. And the quality and duration of your sleep may improve, too.

Practicing the paced breathing once or twice daily for 15 minutes over six weeks leads to the best results. Reasonable results can also be achieved with shorter training sessions.

Over time, your body will learn to create this state of balance and alignment, and you may be able to activate it at will—even in challenging situations. You'll hear more about this when I introduce the Rescue Breath.

Performing Coherence Breathing for even a few seconds before a challenging task can help by reducing performance anxiety and fear of failure and creating a state of sustainable peak performance.

Coherence Breathing is not a relaxation exercise. It can calm and relax when you feel agitated or overexcited, and it can stimulate and activate when you feel low in mood, withdrawn or lack energy. But these effects are experienced as a "bottom-up" cascade of changes, meaning you'll experience them in the lower areas of the brain first, as a physiological response (i.e., decreased tension) before they travel "up" the brain, leading to mental changes (e.g., decreased tension or worry or improved concentration).

Because this follows the way the brain normally processes information, we often feel the effects more quickly and easily than with top-down strategies such as insight and-conscious introspection.

The Breath Pacer

Once you've learned the basic breathing technique with dynamic visualization of sunlight and attention oscillating between body and surrounding, simultaneously focusing on the feeling of gratitude, use the provided audio breath pacer during your Coherence Exercise.

The breath pacer combines slow, deep pacing at 5.5 breathing cycles per minute with brainwave entrainment at gamma 40 Hz embedded in soundscapes and music. Using the breath pacer helps immerse you in the experience and lead you into a state of engagement and balance between focus and relaxation. It also enhances the beneficial physiological changes in breathing and heart, ANS, and brain activity. It's a potent training device that you should use for about six weeks, and then it may be beneficial to continue practicing the exercise without it.

Don't worry if you can't follow all the instructions instantly. With a little practice, you'll grow into this meditation and it will become second nature for you.

Please use headphones when listening to the breath pacer. You can download a folder and choose from breath pacers in different soundscapes (music) as MP3 files from www.bestfutureself.org.

THE POWER OF GRATITUDE

Psychological research has shown that a daily focus on gratitude comes with these benefits:

- Deepens your appreciation for life
- Deepens your appreciation for yourself
- Turns negative emotions into positive emotions
- Improves mood[29]
- Improves health and well-being[30, 31]
- Enhances happiness and satisfaction with life
- Strengthens achievement motivation[32]
- Boosts optimism and self-confidence
- Improves relationships
- Helps you achieve your goals faster

More than a decade of psychological research has shown that practicing gratitude, such as by writing in a gratitude journal, has multiple permanent physiological and psychological health benefits, such as reducing the negative impact of stress, reducing anxiety, and improving mood and sleep.[33]

Focusing on gratitude toward your best future self (your future goals and achievements) is an important part of the of Coherence Training that also enhances heart rate variability and the healthy balance of the autonomic nervous system.

Whenever you remember during the day, embrace the world around you with gratitude. Develop gratitude for the small and big things in life, such as objects in nature or for gifts that life has given you.

EMOTIONS, BREATHING, AND BLOOD CIRCULATION

Anxiety and fear make our breathing shallow and fast and drain the blood from the skin to pool in the abdominal blood vessels. Embarrassment and hot anger can make our breathing involuntarily deep and slow and can dilate the peripheral blood vessels, shown as blushing.

Breathing is the one physiological activity that is half unconscious (you're rarely aware that you're doing it) and half conscious (you're aware of it now). Purposely regulating our breathing can have a powerful effect on the way we manage and change our emotions. When we take a deep breath after a distressing experience, we can feel instant relief from the oppressing emotion.

Whenever we extend our inhalation (breathing in longer than breathing out), we reduce the slowing activity of the PNS and change the balance of our ANS toward sympathetic activity, experiencing stimulation. Whenever we prolong our exhalation, we activate the PNS and experience a sense of calmness, relaxation, and detachment.

This physiological state of balance between sympathetic and parasympathetic activity tends to

- Promote emotional and physical health and well-being.
- Facilitate lasting high performance (cognitive function, motivation, productivity, etc.).
- Optimize social connectedness with other people (emotional regulation).
- Support problem-solving in hard times.
- Improve stress tolerance.

Our bodies can learn this physiological state and reproduce it in demanding situations.

Small clinical trials have shown that Resonant Frequency Training techniques can help control problems like stress, anxiety, anger, depression, panic attacks, attention deficit disorder, asthma, high blood pressure, irritable bowel syndrome, and chronic fatigue syndrome.

Heart rate variability is a measure of how the sympathetic and parasympathetic systems together influence heart rate. It can tell us a lot about the flexibility of our ANS, and in turn, our capacity to control our emotional responses. Effective emotional regulation depends on being able to adjust your physiological response to a changing environment. Heart rate variability measures how well our physiology can be adjusted to meet changing situational demands.

Breathing air into the lungs temporarily blocks the parasympathetic influence on heart rate, producing a heart rate increase. Breathing air out of the lungs restores parasympathetic influence on heart rate, resulting in a heart rate decrease. This rhythmic oscillation in heart rate produced by respiration is called respiratory sinus arrhythmia.

The central autonomic network helps with emotional regulation by adjusting physiological arousal to match the inner and outer environments. The network consists of cortical, limbic, and brainstem components. Its output is transmitted to the sinoatrial node of the heart, among other organs. Heart rate variability reflects, by proxy, an individual's capacity to generate physiological responses that fit their emotional expression.

Slowing down and deepening your breathing to approximately six breathing cycles per minute has a powerful rhythm-enhancing and balancing effect on your autonomic nervous system. It can help give you energy when you're exhausted, but also calm you when you're over-stimulated. This is why our breathing technique is so effective in improving fatigue and exhaustion. It stimulates the balance between strain (sympathetic activity) and recovery (parasympathetic activity). You can enhance the breathing technique's physiological effects even further by focusing on gratitude, joy or confidence (stimulation) at the same time.

TRAINING YOUR HEART RATE VARIABILITY WITH COHERENCE TRAINING CAN HELP

- Improve coherence between the nervous system of brain, heart, and intestines.
- Train your ANS dynamic toward flexibility, rhythm, and balance.
- Reduce the negative impacts of stress and anxiety.
- Build resilience and improve stress tolerance.
- Help you perform well under pressure.
- Help you recover faster.

- Increase mental performance (focus, concentration, memory).
- Improve judgment and decision-making under duress.
- Improve problem-solving in tough situations.
- Reduce impulsivity.
- Decrease frequency of low mood.
- Improve anger management.
- Improve social integration.
- Reduce fatigue.
- Reduce systemic inflammation (a root cause of most "civilizational" diseases).

INSTRUCTIONS

This exercise works best if practiced regularly in a rhythm that fits your lifestyle. Practicing it at the same time each day reinforces its effect. Soon after waking and/or before falling asleep can be particularly effective. Don't try to do the exercises for at least one hour after a main meal.

The Creating Coherence exercise consists of the following parts:

1. Activate and maintain a feeling of gratitude
2. Breathe slowly and deeply
3. Visualize sunlight oscillating between body and periphery

Let's start with the exercise. Please sit comfortably with your arms and legs uncrossed. Become aware of the ground underfoot and the contact your body makes with your chair.

1. Create and sustain the feeling of gratitude

Activate gratitude by imagining for a moment how grateful you are that a desired (future) goal has already become reality. Use positive self-talk to describe to yourself, what it looks and feels like to achieve your goal. Ask yourself why you feel so grateful for having achieved this goal. Once you've created the feeling of gratitude, let go of your thoughts and images and hold on to the feeling while breathing slowly and deeply. If you lose it, you may focus on recreating it in your thoughts while continuing the slow, deep breathing described in the next section.

Select a goal, personal or professional, that you'd like to achieve. This goal can be a new personality trait (such as greater compassion toward yourself and others), a health goal, a career advancement, or a material possession. (See also Exercise 4: A courageous conversation with yourself).

Only choose goals you're confident are achievable and bring no harm to yourself and others. You may start modest and become bolder over time.

Ask yourself how achieving this goal would be good for you and others, and why. Now imagine you've already achieved it and feel deep gratitude for your imagined achievement.

Imagine a concrete life situation that tells you that you've achieved your goal. Imagine it as if it's happening right in front of you. Experience the future as if it's happening now. Make sure that any lack of confidence or fear of failure is replaced during your imagination with gratitude for the achieved.

Now drop your thoughts of your goal and hold on to the feeling of gratitude throughout the exercise. Merge the feeling of gratitude with your deep, slow breathing.

Once you've created the feeling of gratitude, let go of your thoughts and images, and hold on to the feeling while breathing slowly and deeply. If you lose it, you may focus on recreating it in your thinking and imagination while continuing with the slow, deep breathing described in the next section.

You may practice this step for a few days or weeks before adding the next step.

2. Breathe slowly and deeply

- Slow breathing: 5.5 seconds in and 5.5 seconds out (slowly build up the duration).
- Now breathe deeply and slowly through your nose, gently in and out.
- Breathe from your diaphragm upward, filling about 80% of your lungs with air from the bottom up.
- Breathe into the back and front of your lungs.
- As you *inhale*, feel your belly expanding and fill your lungs up to 75% with air.
- As you *exhale*, breathe gently out through your nose as your belly gently contracts. If you can't breathe through your nose, then breathe gently through your mouth.
- Breathe comfortably and smoothly and don't force your breath.
- Once you're comfortable with this exercise, please start using the audio breath pacer ("Coherence breath pacer").

As you match the breath pacer with your breath, maintain deep breathing and focus on your heart and the feeling of deep gratitude while imagining the sunlight expanding into the space around you with every inhalation and contracting back into your body with exhalation.

The breath pacer will help you achieve and maintain the right breathing rhythm. If the pace of the sounds is initially too slow for your liking, follow it with your breathing rhythm for as long as it feels comfortable. Then pause and follow your own rhythm, listening to the tones only, until you're ready to join in again. You may want to alternate for the first few days, until you feel comfortable following the pacer throughout the training.

Please use headphones when listening to the sound files. Use the breath pacer for approximately six to eight weeks. Afterward, you'll be able to practice the whole exercise without any technical help. You can download the breath pacer MP3 files onto your phone from *https://www.bestfutureself.org/breath-pacer-free-download*.

3. Imagine sunlight oscillating between body and periphery

- Once you're able to create and sustain a feeling of gratitude and to follow the breath pacer with your breathing, you may add this dynamic visualization as a third step.
- Imagine your body filled with the golden light, warmth, and vibrance of the sun.
- Imagine your body inside a bubble filled with sunlight, with a diameter of approximately 3 yards (radius of 1.5 yards—this is the extent of the heart's electromagnetic field).
- As you *inhale*, imagine that the golden light, warmth, and vibrance of the sun flow from your body into the periphery, filling the bubble in front and back, left and right, and top and bottom entirely.
- As you *exhale*, imagine that the golden light, warmth, and vibrance of the sun flow from your surrounding bubble into your entire body.
- Try to maintain the feeling of gratitude during breathing and visualization.

Imagine your entire body, every organ, tissue, and cell, filled with the golden light, warmth, and vibrance. Feel the lightness of your body and experience the warmth and the life vibration of the sun within your body, too.

Sustain this flow of light, warmth, and vibrance between body and surroundings throughout the meditation. As you continue breathing and visualizing the moving sunlight, feel deep gratitude for all healing, goodness, beauty, truth, and abundance coming into your life. Continue to breathe golden light, warmth, vibrance, and gratitude in and out.

Practice this exercise once or twice daily in the morning and/or in the evening, but also briefly before and after challenging events.

You may just focus on slowing and deepening your breath and

focusing on gratitude and the sunlight in your body and surroundings for one to five minutes with or without the breath pacer during the day, for example, before and/or after a challenging event.

Practice Coherence Breathing for the duration of 15 minutes at least once daily.

Rescue Breath

You can practice this technique after a distressing experience or to prepare for a challenging event. After practicing your exercise daily for a few weeks, your body will remember the physiological state of coherence and you'll be able to reproduce this physiological state on demand, even in tough situations. You'll then be able to switch from heightened (fight or flight) or reduced (freeze and fold) arousal to a balanced autonomic state (coherence) just by focusing on your heart and taking three to five diaphragmatic breaths at a pace of about five seconds in and five seconds out. For your rescue breath, you won't need any sound files.

Caution: Do not listen to the audio file and do not practice the relaxation training while driving or operating machinery.

TROUBLESHOOTING

Don't worry about being distracted by rising thoughts, feelings, and memories; your exercise will still be effective. Take an interest in these, then send them away and refocus on breathing, gratitude, and your visualization.

1. I lose focus during my training.

Don't worry. With practice, you'll find that your capacity to focus increases. The training is still effective even if you're being distracted as long as you continue with the slow diaphragmatic breathing. Take a brief interest in the distracting thoughts or images, ask them what they want to tell you, then send them away and refocus.

2. I get dizzy while practicing Coherence Training.

If you get dizzy, it's usually because you're hyperventilating, which is an undesirable effect. Please pause the slow, deep breathing immediately and breathe normally. When you've returned to your usual self, restart the training, but breathe less deeply by filling your lungs with less air during the paced breathing cycle.

3. During my training, I experience some discomfort around my heart or some mild palpitations.

This is usually temporary, no major problem, and will stop soon. But if it persists, you may have to stop and/or seek advice from your health professional. It's usually a sign of temporary psycho-physical release.

Caution: Palpitations that are too slow or too fast, or irregular heartbeat combined with dizziness, chest pain, or shortness of breath are signs of a medical emergency and require immediate attention. This condition can develop entirely independent of the training, but in rare cases may coincide with it.

4. I struggle to follow the slow pace of the breath pacer.

If the pace of the sounds is initially too slow for your liking, follow it with your breathing rhythm for as long as it feels comfortable. Then pause and follow your own rhythm, listening to the tones only, until you're ready to join in again. You may alternate for a few days until you feel comfortable following the pace throughout the training.

TIPS FOR PRACTICING COHERENCE TRAINING

1. Be patient.

As you practice this exercise, it helps to try to remain focused and present. Over time, you'll become more and more skilled at maintaining and deepening your focus and relaxation. Be patient with yourself and try to avoid being too goal-oriented with this exercise.

Right away, you'll feel great relief from stress and from the effects of negative emotions when practicing these exercises, but the impact of deep-seated problems on your health and performance may take time to improve or resolve.

2. Set limits.

Don't practice this exercise for more than 15 minutes at a time. Practicing it for 15 minutes at the same time every night and/or morning for six weeks is likely to create a permanent positive effect.

3. Proceed slowly.

During this breathing exercise, at first you may experience feelings, such as mild dizziness. These are often a sign that your perception of your body is changing or coming into sharper focus. Take things slowly and open your eyes during the exercise to regain control and ease the sensations. Most of these sensations are short-lived and tend to disappear entirely with practice.

Some disturbing feelings can also arise, such as fear and anxiety, which may have been previously suppressed. At times, memory images or imaginative pictures can surface as a result of the relaxation process. You may feel sensations of floating and physical weightlessness, increased circulation (warmth), or pins and needles. These feelings are usually mild and transient. They mean that you need to proceed very slowly, gradually adapting to the new psychological and physical experiences. All of these experiences will stop when the exercise ends.

If you notice any dizziness as you practice this breathing technique, try to breathe less deeply—this will stop any signs of hyperventilation.

If you need to, take a break. Don't force any exercise unless it feels natural to you. Perform these exercises gently, and don't put yourself under any pressure.

4. Be relaxed, but alert.

Initially, it's good to do the exercises in a sitting position so you won't fall asleep. But you can also do them standing or lying down, depending on your alertness at the moment and what feels right for you. The aim is to achieve a state of awareness between focus and relaxation.

You may keep your eyes open during the exercise or close them—whichever feels better and more appropriate.

Don't be concerned if you're distracted by any thoughts or memories as you practice this exercise. You may intentionally focus on any randomly appearing thoughts, memories, or images for a while. Give them your undivided attention, then send them away and refocus on your breathing, your heart, and your body periphery.

As you practice every evening and every morning, you'll find it easy to establish this state of focused relaxation at will before, during, and after challenging events during the day.

By focusing on slowing and deepening your breathing and alternating your focus rhythmically between heart and periphery with every breath, you can change the way you respond to challenging situations within a few seconds. This will lead to lower stress levels and sharper performance when the going gets tough.

Make practicing these exercises fun. This is time with and for yourself, and it will benefit your health, your work, and your private life. Coherence Training is not primarily a relaxation exercise; it's a powerful balancing exercise that enhances focus and relaxation and is calming and energizing at the same time. ET reduces the impact of stress and enhances heart rate variability to improve health and performance.

Coherence Training can be helpful

- Before, during, and after challenging situations.
- When you feel anxious, angry, stressed, or down.
- Upon waking to help set the tone for the day.
- Before going to sleep (to help wind down and let go).
- Before an athletic performance (to reduce performance anxiety).

We encourage you to do the training once a day or more, if possible. And, after a while, you can practice resonance training without the breath trainer: focus on slow, deep breathing and on feeling a positive emotion to replace the sounds.

CASE STUDY:
Overcoming Misery

In 2004, a lifetime of negative feelings—principally of anxiety—were precipitated by family circumstances into a much more acute depression with symptoms of sleeplessness, bursts of anger, feelings of a failed and guilty life, and suicidal imaginings.

Now, a year later, my life has been transformed with a much more balanced view of life in all its aspects. In Freud's phrase (though not with his treatment methods), hysterical misery has been replaced with ordinary unhappiness. This residual unhappiness—which is mild rather than severe and does have occasional sunny intervals—is, I think, attributable to a lifelong predisposition to unhappiness springing from childhood and a failure to find ongoing creative activities.

Treatment at my medical practice has consisted of modest doses of antidepressants, now gradually being taken off, together with regular coaching from Dr. Gruenewald in resilience techniques. These have consisted of the breathing exercise (Coherence Training), a combination of relaxation and breathing exercises, and affirmation.

In this process I have developed, with Dr. Gruenewald's flexible approach to treatment, a series of helpful mental pictures (the essence of which came to me unbidden). In these I see a series of colored veils fall from a "diamond" version of myself. They are replaced by more luminously colored positive feelings within the transparent self that arise Phoenix-like from each negative veil, consumed by the fire of love.

Each major negative feeling is replaced by an inwardly and outwardly directed positive feeling.

A red veil of anger is replaced by patience and lovingkindness.

A yellow veil of fear is replaced by courage and trust.

A green veil of envy is replaced by gratitude and empathy.

A white veil of perfectionism is replaced by self-forgiveness and an ability to enjoy the unexpected.

After stopping the antidepressant treatment, I see myself continuing resilience-based exercises, continuing with new creative activities, and making other lifestyle changes as may be necessary.

My treatment has provided a foundation for this future of balanced thinking and feeling.

–L.T., architect, age 62

EXERCISE 2:
Quick Stress Relief

The following exercise combines paced breathing to balance the autonomic nervous system (see Exercise 1: Coherence Training) with a cognitive behavior technique (constructive worry).

Combining the physiological and psychological exercises will let you not only reduce the negative impact of pressure on health, judgment, and decision-making, but also effectively process the issue or event permanently. It helps you neutralize negative emotions and shift toward a sense of being empowered and in control. It offers instant day-to-day stress relief.

BENEFITS

- Relieves stress and extreme emotions instantly.
- Processes challenging situations.
- Prepares for good judgment and decision-making under pressure.
- Enhances performance under pressure.

Step 1 (2 minutes)

- Coherence Breathing (with or without breath pacer and headphones).

- Breathe through your nose, in and out.
- Gently fill your lungs from the diaphragm upward to approximately 75% with air, then gently breathe out.
- If your nose is blocked, you can also breathe through your mouth.
- Maintain balanced breathing throughout the exercise!

Step 2 (30-90 seconds)

Recognize your emotions:
- What makes you feel upset?
- How does it make you feel?
- Name your emotion(s) as precisely as possible.
- Why do you feel this way?

Step 3 (30-90 seconds)

Behavioral response:
- How will you respond to a similar situation in the future? What will you do about it? Write it down.
- Imagine for a moment how it will look and feel when you've implemented your intention.

EXERCISE 3:
In-Step Technique

The In-Step Technique is about mindful detachment and connecting at will.

BENEFITS

- Facilitates in-depth learning from past experiences
- Processes and shifts negative emotions
- Helps you change to and rehearse new behavioral response patterns
- Improves your performance
- Prevents build-up of overstrain
- Develops flexibility, equanimity, creativity, and self-determination
- Maintains the overview
- Helps you effectively recover from strain
- Empowers you to meet similar challenging situations with flexibility, equanimity, creativity, and self-determination

Imagine you're on the dance floor of a ballroom with balconies, and after having enjoyed yourself for a while, you ask your partner to go with you onto the balcony. You climb the stairs to the next floor and step right onto the balcony overlooking the dance floor. Standing there and looking down gives you a different perspective: you've gained overview. For example, you see your friends dancing, the clothes they're wearing, where the musicians are playing, where the drinks are being served, etc. Now, imagine you're able to do something very unusual: although you're standing on the balcony, look back in your imagination to when you were dancing on the ballroom floor. See yourself dancing with your partner, but from the balcony perspective—looking down onto yourself, becoming your own observer.

This witness or onlooker consciousness is far from alien to us; it's quite the opposite. As we look back and remember, we may experience these past events in two opposite manners: we either experience ourselves from inside our body, or we see ourselves in our memory like we're looking a picture, from outside. The way we relate to the past event depends on our perspective:

1. If we experience ourselves from inside our body and see the event through our own eyes during the act of remembering, we relive and re-experience the event with all its feelings and emotions attached. This experience of reliving the event makes it even more tangible for us and heightens our emotional response to it—even though it's in the past. This is one of the reasons we should avoid remembering traumatic events without therapeutic support, as reliving an event may make the impact of its trauma worse.

2. If we see ourselves from the outside in our memory, we're disconnected and removed: we review the event rather than relive it. As we review it and ask ourselves what we experienced at the time, we create something like a third-person account; we become our own observer. This helps us process the event and neutralizes any negative emotions, as we will see.

We don't always have to be one with events and our emotions, but can instead become the observer of our own mind and consciousness

EXERCISE 3: IN-STEP TECHNIQUE

and describe events and emotions objectively. Experiencing this reality allows us to develop calm detachment in the most challenging times. We can deliberately practice remembering with inner detachment, which is part of our natural, day-to-day experience. Further, we can turn it into a powerful technique that gives us a stronger sense of identity, even in very demanding situations. This lets us reduce personal bias, strengthens the quality of our judgment and decision-making, protects us from growing bitter, and can even prevent trauma during catastrophe.[34]

Different people view a challenge in different ways, and even the same person may see it differently under different life circumstances. The perception of the challenge depends on our angle of view and our perspective. The perspective we take impacts our emotions, which in turn influence our judgment and decision-making.

We experience the phenomenon of shifting perspective best when we look at a challenging situation again after a good night's sleep. For example, suppose you write an email about a situation that's bothering you while in a state of strong emotional involvement. Afterward, you decide you don't want to send it right away, but would rather sit on it for a little while. The next day, after a good night's sleep, you read the email again. Suddenly the situation doesn't seem so overwhelming anymore, and you feel relieved that you didn't send it after all.

Our In-Step Technique helps deepen the capacity to detach and connect with challenging life situations at will, as a foundation for emotional and physical health and performance. This exercise is physiologically supported by the Coherence Breathing exercise, which creates a balance between attachment and detachment.

The Review part of the exercise helps neutralize negative emotions attached to the experience, such as fear of failure, disappointment, anger, and frustration. The Preview is a form of mental rehearsal that strengthens the will to implement your goals and replaces fear of failure with confidence and gratitude.

We can often move from one activity to the next more effectively if we process the previous experience first. Processing one thing at a time also allows us to critically reflect on and understand our past experiences (Step out), then mentally rehearse and prepare a better response to similar events in the future (Step in). To boost your ability to manage a high workload and/or frequent transitions, try this technique.

STEPS IN THE TECHNIQUE

Step out

- Stay calm and detached; mentally observe yourself and your environment

Make sense

- Make sense of the past
- Set a goal for the future

Step in

- Explore, imagine (mentally rehearse), and appreciate
- Select a past event or future goal you would like to work on

INSTRUCTIONS

Step 1: Review (Stepping out)

- Focus on calmness. Breathe slowly and deeply with a focus on calmness. Maintain this breathing throughout the exercise.
- Observe and describe the situation and your emotions. Describe the experience and name your emotions. What have you experienced? How did it feel at the time?
- Ask yourself how best to relate to this event.

Step 2: Contemplation (Making sense)

- What can you learn from your experience about yourself, others, and the situation?
- What would you like to achieve and why?
- How would you like to conduct yourself in the future?

Step 3: Mental rehearsal (Stepping in)[35]

- Appreciate the situation as one you'll be able to learn from. If the event was traumatic, imagine looking back later and identifying what you may have gained from this experience.
- Explore how you would like to relate to a similar event in the future. Use your "realistic imagination" to explore your options.
- Imagine, with confidence and determination, how you'll handle a similar event in the future. Experience yourself inside your body and engage your bodily senses.
- Imagine having achieved your goal now and feel a strong sense of gratitude.

EXERCISE 4:
A Courageous Conversation with Myself (Positive Self-Talk)

"After examining the philosophies, the theories, and the practiced methods of influencing human behavior, I was shocked to learn the simplicity of that one small fact: You will become what you think about most; your success or failure in anything, large or small, will depend on your programming—what you accept from others, and what you say when you talk to yourself. It is no longer a success theory; it is a simple but powerful fact. Neither luck nor desire has the slightest thing to do with it. It makes no difference whether we believe it or not. The brain simply believes what you tell it most. And what you tell it about you, it will create. It has no choice."

–*Shad Helmstetter, What to Say When You Talk to Yourself*[36]

BENEFITS

- Creates purpose, ethos, enthusiasm, confidence, and strong motivation[37]
- Inspires and enables you and others to change and to act
- Helps you understand and transform risks, obstacles, and resistance
- Improves performance[38, 39]

Finding balance and alignment among our thinking (cognition), feeling (emotions), and willing (acting) requires conscious awareness and willful control of our emotions and feelings. An important way to do that is to develop "heart thinking."

Developing heart thinking can be done through a courageous conversation with ourselves. Have you ever quietly talked to yourself? Inner conversations are often fragmented: "Oh, dear, why me again?" Or they can be coherent, like an inner exploration.

The difference between thinking about something and exploring it in a quiet conversation with myself is that, in conversation, I penetrate my thoughts with feelings and intentions. This process can make me feel excited and courageous, and I'm able to share this enthusiasm.[40]

As I explore a meaningful question in a quiet conversation with myself, I become truly engaged and align my thinking, feeling, and willing.

In fact, I believe that influential and inspiring people have frequent and fluent conversations with themselves.

The starting point of effective heart thinking is heartfelt questions that explore our sense of purpose and future goals. Instead of just going with the flow of life, we need to set goals and create purpose. For example, we can ask ourselves questions like these:

- Where would I like to be in my personal or professional development in a year's time?
- How would I like my relationship with my partner to look in one year?
- When I'm 70 years old and look back on my life, what would I like to see in order to be able to say, "This has been a life well lived"?

The answers to these vital, purpose-creating questions can't be found with our normal day-to-day intellect. They demand a heart thinking that reaches into the future and unites thinking, feeling, and willing.

EXERCISE 4: A COURAGEOUS CONVERSATION WITH MYSELF (POSITIVE SELF-TALK)

Heart thinking helps us develop comprehensibility and meaningfulness for life, and by exploring the path, obstacles, and strategies on the path toward your goals, you also develop manageability.

Aaron Antonovsky, a medical sociologist, discovered that people who were unusually healthy many years after surviving concentration camp internment had developed three skills before the age of 25: comprehensibility (understanding), meaningfulness (making sense of one's life and life circumstances), and manageability. In his research, he noted these skills as crucial for maintaining good health despite adverse circumstances.

The good news is, even if we haven't developed these skills yet, heart thinking can become the tool that helps us do so. Further, it can help us deepen them. This is how I advise you to practice:

First, formulate essential questions and then answer them in writing. Once this task is completed, explore the questions one by one in your mind. You might imagine being interviewed by your best friend, with your friend asking the questions and you answering them. Of course, this conversation can be anything between a monologue and a dialogue.

Why do I call this self-conversation courageous? As you practice, you'll encounter truthfulness, which may conflict with your dearly held opinions and convictions. And this discrepancy can be unsettling at times. Facing it requires courage. A participant in one of my workshops gave the following feedback: "I suddenly realize how much I've been lying every day."

Exploring your life questions through heart thinking can bring us in touch with our own source of truth and life purpose. This can be uncomfortable if our life is unaligned with our own inner sense of purpose or if we just follow the demands of the world around us rather than setting direction from within. But it's an inner adventure well worth attempting.

I will now give you examples of how to formulate your questions, but please be aware that these are only examples and the technique can be applied to any area of your life. You'll also want to formulate your questions as specifically and relevantly as possible for yourself.

EXAMPLE QUESTIONS
My Favorite Project

- What would I like to achieve?
- Why would I like to achieve that?
- How will achieving my goal affect me and others?
- How will it make me feel?
- What are the obstacles?
- What could go wrong? (risks)
- What's the worst credible outcome?
- What's the best possible outcome?
- How will I go about it to achieve my goals and overcome the obstacles?
- Where can I get help?

INSTRUCTIONS

1. Formulate your questions in writing.
2. Write down the answers to the questions.
3. Pick one particular question and explore it in a silent conversation with yourself. Focus not only on your thoughts, but also on your feelings and intentions.
4. Feel your breathing slow and deepen during this process. You're now thinking, feeling, and willing within your own heart.
5. Don't get disheartened if you feel distracted and it takes time to get into the flow. You may want to keep your eyes open during this process initially. With a little practice, you'll succeed.

Once you master the exercise, you may want to do it from time to time, maybe once every one to four weeks, to explore the important questions in your life.

EXERCISE 4: A COURAGEOUS CONVERSATION WITH MYSELF (POSITIVE SELF-TALK)

FOLLOWING UP WITH THE GRATITUDE TECHNIQUE

Follow this exercise with a Gratitude part of the Coherence exercise (see the step: "Create and sustain the feeling of gratitude" in Exercise 1: 'Coherence Training').

Imagine having achieved your (future) goal now, develop a deep sense of gratitude for having achieved it, and write down five reasons you feel grateful for having achieved it. Use imagination and positive self-talk to describe yourself the nature of what you consider as success.

Then create a list of up to three actions you commit to doing in order to move toward your goal. The next day, start implementing these self-chosen actions.

Tip

Practice this once or twice a day over the next 3 weeks; this is how long it takes to create the new neuropathways for successful change.

Strengthen Your Willpower and Attract Favorable Circumstances

1. Review (Stepping out)

Briefly review your past behavior and situations related to your goal, but also ways you may have prevented yourself from achieving it. Do this from the perspective of the observer. Step out and look at yourself as a dispassionate observer in the process of reviewing the past.

2. Contemplation

Ask yourself why you conducted yourself in a certain way and try to make sense of the circumstances. Then ask yourself how you'd like to achieve your goal and what motivates you. How would achieving or not achieving your goal impact you and others, and how would you want to go about dealing with the obstacles?

3. Preview (Stepping in)

Now imagine taking strong actions. Imagine doing your activities that lead toward overcoming obstacles and successfully achieving your goals. Picture yourself from inside your body.

You can support this technique of mental rehearsal by applying Coherent Breathing (without visualization of light). Create a strong feeling of gratitude for the actions that bring you closer to success. Whenever you feel a fear of failure or lack of confidence, or experience yourself outside your body in your visualization, stop the mental rehearsal and re-establish your slow, deep breathing. Focus on the feeling of gratitude and enter your body by imagining the experience of touch, pressure, and movement. Then refocus on mentally rehearsing the work toward your goal. As you do this, feel the connection with your body and maintain the feeling of gratitude for the work that leads to achieving your goal. Repeat this process until you can mentally rehearse with gratitude, bodily connection, and freedom from fear.

You can also imagine having achieved your goal now and feel a strong sense of gratitude for having done so (please see also In-Step Technique).

4. Gratitude for future achievements

Imagine having achieved your (future) goal now, develop a deep sense of gratitude for having achieved it, and write down five reasons you feel grateful for having achieved it. Picture, what it looks and feels like, to have achieved your goal. Use imagination and positive self-talk.

5. Make a list of what you have to do and take decisive action

Then create a list of up to three actions you commit to doing in order to move toward your goal. The next day, start implementing these self-chosen actions. You may want to repeat the exercise for the same goal a few times.

CASE STUDY:
Living with a Demanding Mother

I am 43 years old, married with three children (now aged 13, 15, and 3). I work as an electronics engineer, developing and designing products for computers.

My mother has been living with the family for the past four years. This decision was based on a certain necessity but also on genuine mutual fondness. The first two years went well, and everybody was pleased with the arrangement. This has changed dramatically over the past two years.

When I first saw Dr. Gruenewald, I felt emotionally drained and physically exhausted. I felt that my enjoyment of life had been lost. What kept me going was my sense of duty toward my family. I felt that I was just going through the motions of life, although I wasn't sure whether there was much point in that at all.

I didn't want to end my life, but I would have liked to just fall asleep and not awaken again. I had stopped enjoying activities I previously enjoyed, for example, socializing with friends. I believed the cause of all my problems was the drastic change in my relationship with my mother.

My mother had become increasingly demanding, constantly complaining and interfering with our family life. She was insensitive to everyone else's needs, and intrusive.

I blamed myself for the fact that my wife and family found life with my mother (and with me!) increasingly difficult. The only one who still liked having his grandmother around was my three-year-old son, who has a sunny disposition and seems happy anywhere.

Over the last few months I had become irritable, often very angry and short-tempered, full of guilt and confusion about my own behavior. I avoided my mother wherever I could as a measure of self-protection.

I had been feeling very resentful toward her, partly because I started to remember a lot of negative experiences from the past and because I blamed her for all our current problems.

She didn't show any understanding for my very busy and demanding work, nor for the circumstances of my wife or teenage children. I felt trapped and couldn't see a way out. I also felt depressed and developed other health problems.

I found it difficult to speak to my friends about the home situation because I thought all my problems might sound petty and ridiculous. I felt ashamed and worried that they might consider me a complete failure and unable to deal with my problems adequately.

All this has impacted not only my relationship with my wife and children, but also my work, and that was what finally drove me to consult a doctor. I had developed sleep problems, high blood pressure, and frequent headaches, and I kept worrying about my more or less constant dull stomachache.

Dr. Gruenewald took time to listen to me and asked me to come again for a 30-minute appointment. He arranged for some medical investigations (blood tests) that, besides increased cholesterol and slightly high blood pressure, all turned out normal.

At the second consultation, Dr. Gruenewald invited me to see him for a one-to-one coaching session using the adaptive resilience approach. He suggested teaching me techniques that would empower me to cope better with my life situation and social relationships and that could help improve my low mood.

I was motivated to give it a go as I saw a possibility of avoiding medication and talk therapy, which I wasn't so keen on anyway. Dr.

CASE STUDY: LIVING WITH A DEMANDING MOTHER

Gruenewald suggested that counseling or medication may still be needed but agreed to pursue the Adaptive Resilience approach first.

In my first adaptive resilience session, Dr. Gruenewald gave me an overview of the approach and its clinical background. He introduced the Coherence Exercise to me and suggested that I practice it at least once daily for 10 minutes, but more frequently if possible.

He advised me to practice the breathing technique once or twice daily for 15 minutes. Within a few days of practicing the breathing technique, I experienced a new sense of inner calmness, not only during the exercise but also, at least at times, throughout the day.

After about two weeks, I realized that I had been significantly more relaxed in my communication with all members of my family, including my mother. My wife confirmed that change.

I started to feel less anxious and irritable and became able to stay calm in many of the challenging situations. I had been practicing about twice a day for at least 15 minutes and had enjoyed it and considered it my personal quality time. I feel that as soon as I practiced controlled regular breathing, I experienced a deep sense of calmness and relaxation.

My low mood hadn't improved much, though. I still felt low most of the time when I saw Dr. Gruenewald again two weeks after the previous consultation. But I was encouraged by the progress I had made with my fears and irritability and I felt generally more hopeful. During this session, Dr. Gruenewald introduced the Courageous Conversation exercise. He advised me to spend only up to 20 minutes on the Coherence exercise and then to move on to this new exercise.

Practicing the Courageous Conversation with myself, I started to recollect very recent situations. In the evening, I looked back to encounters with my mother during the day. I tried to remember each situation as vividly as possible. I tried to visualize my mother's and my own gestures, facial expressions, spoken and unspoken words, and feelings in the situation.

I learned how to cope with the feelings attached to the memories by continuing with balanced breathing and feeling deep calmness.

The feelings I experienced at the time were anger, annoyance, frustration, and sadness. I learned how to ease these feelings and look at the situation in a more detached way. Moving on to the next step of the exercise, I learned to develop feelings of compassion for myself, something I've never done before in my life. The image of the hurt child within me was a great help. I then moved on to mentally rehearsing difficult life situations by picturing myself in difficult times with my mother and finding calmness, caring, and strength to resolve these situations amicably.

Having practiced it for a while, I started to apply this exercise to my mother. I reflected on some of the personal traits in her that I really appreciate and allowed myself to create and experience feelings of appreciation for her. For example, I admire her patience in dealing with my children.

In the next step, I faced the difficult sides of our relationship, but this time not criticizing, but rather trying to understand her behavior and reactions from her perspective and by reflecting on her own difficult childhood experiences.

From here it wasn't too difficult anymore to develop a sense of compassion for my mother as I recognized how little she seemed to be in charge of her own behavior and emotional responses. As I experienced compassion for her and her current life situation, I extended it to her "victims," too (my family and myself). I ended the exercise by asking myself how to best respond to this life situation in order to find a solution to the conflict.

I practiced this exercise about four times and experienced a significant change within myself after a few days. I learned to develop a sense of acceptance not only for her, but for my failures too. I learned to see our whole situation in a different light.

The change of attitude toward myself and my mother changed my perspective on our problems, and now I can respond to her better even in challenging daily situations. For example, I can feel my mother's pain and concern and understand the motives for her actions. I have

CASE STUDY: LIVING WITH A DEMANDING MOTHER

gradually come to recognize that she has no intention of harming anyone.

Also, surprisingly, it hasn't been too difficult to replace blaming my mother, other family members, or myself with positive assertiveness, understanding, and forgiveness. Of course, this works better on some days than others, but I also realized there are issues that need more work and others that now seem to be resolving almost effortlessly.

What surprised me most was that, although I had never talked to my mother about the exercises I'd been doing, she seemed to have been changing too, opening up and showing more interest in the family's life again.

My relationship with my family has improved as well and I feel optimistic about the future. The physical symptoms have eased up, in step with the disappearing tension.

I've made the Coherence Breathing and Courageous Conversation exercises a regular part of my life now. I've learned to use and adapt them to my own needs for other situations, for example, to improve difficult relationships at work. I do seem to get on a lot better with family, friends, and colleagues now.

–B.R., engineer, age 43

EXERCISE 5:
Mindful Nature Observation

BENEFITS

- Enhances your emotional and physical health and well-being[41]
- Improves focus and concentration
- Suspends judgment
- Enhances depth of perception
- Enhances health and vitality
- Connects you with nature on a deeper level
- Develops perception, intuitive insight, and understanding
- Teaches you to live stronger in the moment

For many people, the relationship with nature has been affected by the growth of technology. We spend more time indoors and in front of screens: smartphones, tablets, computers, and TVs. For many children, human interactions are replaced by screen time.

Nature deprivation—or Nature Deficit Disorder—may have a serious impact on our mental and emotional health.[42] Spending more quality time in nature, gardening, walking, or observing nature seems to have a strong positive effect on stress levels and mental health.[43]

With the help of the exercise below, you'll enter fully into a state of perception with undivided attention, leading to an extension of your perceptions.

By suspending judgment, you can open yourself fully to the object you're observing. This allows perceived impressions to resonate deep within you, creating thoughts, feelings, and images that rise up as an inner response. The insights you achieve through this mode of perception are usually deeper, more intuitive, and therefore more in tune with the object of observation.

Goethe's scientific nature research is based on this methodology, which is known as Goethean observation.[44]

Observe nature to maintain your mental and emotional health. This exercise can take up to five minutes.

INSTRUCTIONS

- Slow down and deepen your breathing.
- Focus entirely on a natural object (for example, a plant, an animal, the sky, or the ocean), absorbing all details and engaging all your senses (sight, sound, smell, taste, warmth, touch, movement, balance).
- Avoid any judgment or reflection during this moment. Focus on sensory perceptions rather than on the thoughts or inner images that arise within you. Suppress any thoughts and images as they arise and re-focus on perceiving.
- Take a warm and deep interest in all the details while observing.
- After a few minutes of undivided attention, focus on your inner response and become aware of the feelings, thoughts, and images, that have been generated within you by the object of observation.

This exercise offers a means to go beyond our narrow, self-focused experiences

EXERCISE 6:
Active Listening

The goal of active listening is to suspend judgment in favor of unconditional regard. In other words, we refrain from forming opinions and simply listen.

BENEFITS

- Improves communication[45]
- Deepens your perceptions of and insight into other people's thoughts, feelings, and intentions[46, 47]
- Establishes excellent rapport[48]
- Improves relationships, builds trust, builds team coherence[49]

Establishing excellent relationships requires the capacity to sincerely listen and understand, to genuinely appreciate, and to communicate well. As you suspend your judgment and deepen your interest while listening to the other person, you'll improve your relationships.

When suspending judgment, you can open yourself to the object of your observation. This allows your impressions to resonate within you, creating thoughts, feelings, and images that rise up as an inner response. The insights you achieve through this mode of perception will be deeper, more intuitive, and therefore more in tune with the object of observation.

Extending your perception to develop an intuitive understanding of your surroundings, both human and nonhuman, will considerably reduce stress, enhancing your health and vitality, and can create a deep sense of joy and connectedness with life.

Admitting how strongly our view of the world is affected by more or less conscious judgments and biases we have developed from our past experiences is the first step toward overcoming them. Anybody who tries to listen to someone with a different worldview or political opinion knows how hard it is to silence the inner judge. In fact, when you start to practice this exercise, it'll take a lot of energy to actively suppress any surfacing judgments and enter a process of pure and active listening. This process will allow the thoughts, feelings, and intentions of the other person take center stage in our consciousness without being interrupted by our own.

So, active listening requires an act of willful selflessness, the capacity to let go of our own thoughts, feelings, and intentions in order to become one with the consciousness of the other person, walk in their shoes, and see the world through their eyes. Any honest and truthful effort on this path trains our capacity to love and to develop intuition. The activity is one of encountering the other person in a childlike way, full of burning interest and awe. I imagine what it would mean for our relationships if we could maintain this deep interest, curiosity, and devotion even for people we have already known for a long time. We might see our partners, relatives, and friends as if meeting them for the first time.

Here are three steps or levels of this process:

- **Being open-minded** by actively suspending judgment is the first step on this path toward keeping our relationships essential and alive.
- **Being open-hearted** lets the warmth of compassion, gratitude, and love enter the relationship.
- **Being open-willed** lets us perceive the developmental needs of

EXERCISE 6: ACTIVE LISTENING

the other person and how we can help meet them. Our inner strength and goodness develop as we put the deeper needs of the other person above our own in thought and action.

Otto Scharmer refers to these three "open" qualities when he describes that we need to transcend our "ego-system" and find solutions to the most burning questions of our time.[50]

Active listening with an open mind, heart, and will is truly transformative for both the listener and the person who is perceived and received in that way. It's an essential part of any deeper therapeutic process, also described as empathy. Humanistic psychotherapist Carl Rogers and his pupils identified this process as the core element of any therapeutic transformation.[51]

Rogers asserted that empathy helps clients

- Pay attention and value their experiencing.
- See earlier experiences in new ways.
- Modify their views of themselves, others, and the world.
- Increase their confidence in making choices and pursuing a course of action.

According to Jeanne Watson, 60 years of research have consistently demonstrated that empathy is the most powerful determinant of client progress in therapy. She puts it this way: "Therapists need to be able to be responsively attuned to their clients and to understand them emotionally as well as cognitively. When empathy is operating on all three levels—interpersonal, cognitive, and affective—it is one of the most powerful tools therapists have at their disposal."[52]

As we'll see, the active listening process doesn't listen only for the content that's being expressed, but also seeks to perceive emotions, feelings, and intentions. It looks to understand the other person's authenticity and alignment of thinking, feeling, and willing. At its root, it's not an act of interpretation, but of pure, intentional perception.

And it includes not just the understanding of concepts, but also the perception of nonverbal elements such as pitch, volume, and flow of voice and expression through posture, gesture, and mimic—tone of voice and body language.

Every conversation should live in the dual "rhythmic" process of intense and pure listening, in which we try to be one with the other person and then be completely with ourselves in processing and making sense of what was expressed. That's why we won't abolish judgment, just suspend it.

Instead of multitasking, processing information while receiving it, we separate these processes and intentionally practice one activity at a time. In conversations, we usually tend to listen, and at the same time remember past experiences, analyze what it all means for us, and work out how we can use the new information later.

Nobody is good at multitasking, and in fact, instead of multitasking, our mind usually engages in serial tasks, which means it constantly switches from one activity to the other. If this switching isn't slowed down a lot, then we don't perform any of these activities very well. Imagine you had to listen to a talk and answer an email simultaneously; how would this multitasking affect the quality of both activities?

Giving undivided attention to listening before processing the information gives strength and depth to each of these activities. You'll intuit the other person profoundly, creating a much deeper connection, insight, and rapport. This can transform our human encounters into therapeutic processes and acts of love. Below are the steps of this exercise.

INSTRUCTIONS

- Deepen and slow your breathing and focus on calmness and appreciation.
- Focus on the other person: their voice, pitch, and rhythm of speech, and their breathing, expression, and gestures.
- Focus on not just *what* is being said, but also *how* it's being said.

EXERCISE 6: ACTIVE LISTENING

- Avoid and suppress any immediate judgment or emotional response.
- After carefully listening without judgment, focus for a short time on your thoughts and feelings about the person.
- Recognize the other person's feelings, needs, and intentions.
- While responding, re-focus on the person.

In daily life, you may pick the conversations that are suitable to practice active listening. The duration of undivided attention may vary depending on the situation (from 30 seconds up to five minutes). Allow yourself time to let the experience reverberate within you and to form your judgments (after listening with undivided attention).

In my years of experience as a GP and clinical specialist, I've experienced again and again how powerfully transformative this active listening can be for myself and the person I'm listening to, never mind the original purpose of the consultation. It builds the necessary trust, rapport, and transformative relationship. And I also experience the positive effects in my personal relationships whenever I practice this exercise.

CASE STUDY:
Preparing for a Difficult Meeting

The day after I took part in an introductory workshop on the Resilience techniques, I attended a meeting about which I was very concerned. I knew a difficult issue would be discussed, and I felt a huge resentment about it. I was worried that my resentment would get the better of me and that I would create an angry scene. In addition, a manager would be present whom I had confronted about lying once before, fueling my resentment even further.

Ten minutes before the meeting, I sat down quietly and did the breathing technique and reminded myself of my experience with the Active Listening exercise. That took five minutes. I then had another five minutes to "come back into the world" and make my way into the meeting room.

Once there, I was amazed at how calm I was and how much genuine appreciation I experienced for the manager's general attitude and professionalism.

When I spoke, it felt as if the resentment had simply vanished. Instead I was clear, articulate, and assertive when I stated a request. The words just came without premeditation and it was only when I actually spoke that I realized my request meant that it would be difficult for the manager to be "economical with the truth" at a later point. My request was accepted.

Since then I have practiced the resilience exercises on a daily basis. As a result, I am generally calmer and able to quietly and assertively ask for what I want as well as set boundaries. Until now I have had great difficulties with both of these.

–M.F., accountant, age 49

EXERCISE 7:
Transforming Difficult Relationships

BENEFITS

- Assists in defining the outcome (goal)
- Acknowledges risks and obstacles
- Develops a strategy[53]
- Mentally rehearses being at your best in challenging circumstances
- Helps you become receptive, persuasive, and assertive

The process of transforming difficult relationships involves two components: developing emotional intelligence and learning to emphasize positive rather than negative emotions.

DEVELOPING EMOTIONAL INTELLIGENCE

- Acknowledging and managing your emotions
- Acknowledging and managing the emotions of others

SHIFTING FROM NEGATIVE TO POSITIVE EMOTIONAL STATES

- Maintaining calmness in critical situations
- Creating appreciation for yourself and others

- Developing and maintaining a sense of purpose
- Being confident
- Being open-minded
- Being open-hearted
- Being open-willed

INSTRUCTIONS

You can apply four main activities to transform difficult human relationships.

1. Review (Let go of resentments)

When processing difficult human encounters, it can be helpful to review challenging situations from an observer perspective (balcony view), picturing yourself from outside and reviewing (picturing) the past situation in a dispassionate way. Asking yourself how you felt at the time can highlight your emotions toward this past situation and neutralize them by naming them as precisely as possible. Be aware that, for example, behind anger stand more differentiated emotions, such as disappointment, impatience, hurt, or frustration. You may want to write the actual situation down and your emotions toward the situation or relationship at hand. Just try to review past events that represent the relationship issues by seeing yourself in your memory from outside. **Do not relive these situations, but only review them.** This will let you process the attached emotions, understand and accept them, and let them go. In fact, it's a very effective way of processing and neutralizing your negative emotions.

If you struggle to stay emotionally calm and detached, then practice Coherence Breathing as you review your memory or memories. The slow, deep breathing, with or without the breath pacer, may act as a safety anchor to prevent you from becoming overly upset or retraumatized.

Whenever you start to feel overwhelmed by extreme emotions, just stop the review. Focus on your breathing, breath pacer, and soundscape, and develop a sense of calmness and equanimity.

Once you've done this, then the issue at hand will stop hurting and upsetting you. You'll feel safe and protected and a bit actively detached (at will) from the issue at hand. When similar situations arise later, they won't affect you as much anymore and you'll instinctively know how to respond. This is Stage 1 of the process.

2. Contemplation (Courageous Conversation with yourself)

Once you've neutralized the negative emotions attached to your relationship, you're ready to enter this silent conversation with yourself. You can do this in writing *and* in quiet self-talk. You'll ask yourself a number of courageous questions and explore them.

For example: Why have these difficulties developed? What have I contributed to them? What's the worst credible future outcome? What's the potential learning and inner growth that I (we) can derive from this suffering? If things developed as well as they could, what would I want this relationship to turn into (best credible outcome)? What are the steps I would take to improve the situation in my and other people's interest?

Ask yourself under what circumstances you can develop compassion for yourself and the other person involved? If you are able to, do so. Are you also able to forgive yourself and the other person? If, yes, try to do so. Don't worry if (self-)compassion and forgiveness are not yet possible for you. Over time, they may become possible and you'll instantly feel incredible relief, empowerment, and liberation.

3. Mental rehearsal (Creative visualization)

Once you've completed the first two steps, it's time to move on to Mental Rehearsal. This technique, frequently used in sports psychology to prepare for peak performance, can help you develop the practical skills you need to change the situation for the better. It also promotes motivation and endurance.

Now imagine yourself in a challenging encounter with the person or people you've struggled to relate well to. Imagine how, within a challenging situation, you stay calm, confident, and insightful and act out of your best skills and intentions. As you mentally rehearse (visualize) this scenario, try to stay inside your body at all times. In fact, try to imagine the bodily sensations you'd have in this situation, such as touch experiences, experiences of movement and deep pressure (like feeling the contact your body makes with a chair, feeling the ground underfoot while walking, or feeling the tension in your calf muscles while climbing stairs or walking uphill). If you instead feel yourself disconnecting from your body and seeing yourself from outside, or if you feel anxiety, fear, dread, anger, or any other negative emotion during the exercise, stop the visualization instantly and focus on your breathing, making it slow and deep. Once you've reestablished a sense of calmness and confidence, you can start rehearsing again, maintaining the sense of connection with your body and a sense of calmness and confidence.

You may find it helpful to practice your Coherence Breathing and use the breath pacer simultaneously (of course, without the visualization of sunlight) while you practice mental rehearsal. Once you've mentally rehearsed the future event successfully, pretending as if it's happening now, develop a strong sense of gratitude for your goals and achievements.

If you struggle to imagine yourself inside your body during mental rehearsal, try the following: imagine walking up a hill or climbing a staircase with your eyes closed while carrying heavy objects, like a stack of books. As you do this, feel the sensations of touch, pressure, movement, and balance as lively as possible. When repeatedly practiced, this exercise will soon enable you to stay connected with your body throughout mental rehearsal. Research into the mental rehearsing exercise has shown that the process of skill-building is far enhanced when you imagine yourself inside your body while mentally rehearsing.

4. Active listening and observing (Suspend judgment with unconditional regard)

Now that you're sufficiently prepared and protected, you'll be able to enter active listening and observation when meeting the person in question. Open your senses and take in with deep interest what you can hear and see of the other person, temporarily suspending all judgment. Suppress any thoughts that enter your mind and focus only on listening and observing even the smallest details: their breath, movements, gestures, pitch of voice, melody of voice, rhythm, pace of speaking, etc. Then let these impressions reverberate within you and ask yourself what you've observed and what it means. As you meet the other person with an open mind and heart and without judgment, you create deep rapport and help them work on their own issues. As a result, your relationship is likely to improve.

Admittedly, this is a lengthy process and you won't want to apply it to all your relationships. But if you apply it to the important relationships in your life, it may lead to a profound transformation.

WORKING WITH DIFFICULT RELATIONSHIPS

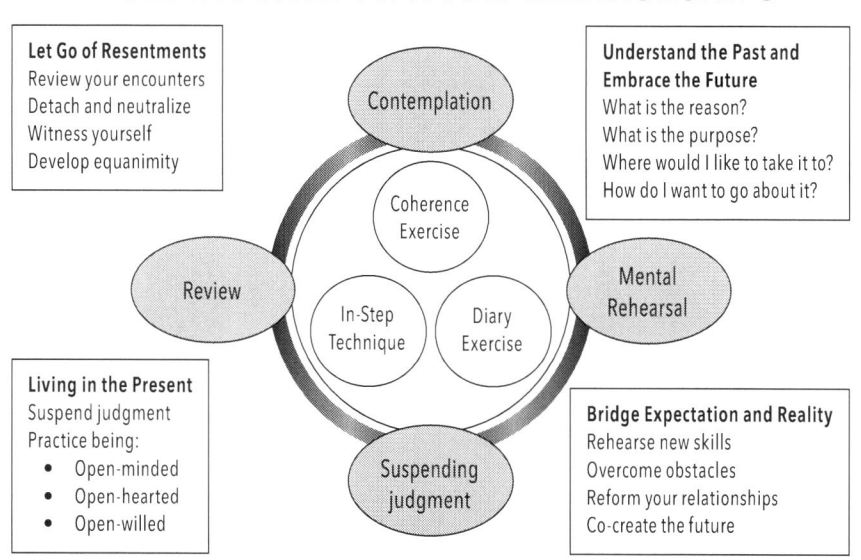

Let Go of Resentments
Review your encounters
Detach and neutralize
Witness yourself
Develop equanimity

Understand the Past and Embrace the Future
What is the reason?
What is the purpose?
Where would I like to take it to?
How do I want to go about it?

Living in the Present
Suspend judgment
Practice being:
- Open-minded
- Open-hearted
- Open-willed

Bridge Expectation and Reality
Rehearse new skills
Overcome obstacles
Reform your relationships
Co-create the future

Contemplation
Review
Mental Rehearsal
Suspending judgment

Coherence Exercise
In-Step Technique
Diary Exercise

CASE STUDY:
Frustration of a Teenager

I was in my last year of high school and found it extremely stressful. I wanted to study law and needed very good results. I was always a good student but was at odds with my history teacher. I felt that he hated me, wanted me to fail, but was himself incompetent in some areas of the subject. We often used to have words, where I felt I was in the right, but my teacher just wouldn't admit it. He was out to get me!

I was so worked up and frustrated that it had a negative effect on my attitude toward school. I became extremely bad-tempered and started falling out with my sister, who claims I had become unbearable. I felt that nobody understood the pressure I was under, blamed family and friends for not caring, and talked about giving it all up and traveling to get rid of them all. But I also felt ill all the time and wondered whether I had the strength for traveling on the cheap.

I decided to see Dr. Gruenewald only as a (last) favor to my parents, and in the beginning, I wasn't very engaged at all. I must have come across as impatient and arrogant. As our conversation continued, I felt safe to open up and poured out my grievances. After a while I even enjoyed the conversation, as I realized that I wasn't being criticized or blamed.

I agreed to start with some relaxation exercises to help me calm down because I somehow felt sad and frustrated that I kept losing my temper with the people I liked and cared about.

A week or two after I began practicing the exercises almost daily, my sleep started to improve even though I hadn't even realized its sleep quality had deteriorated over the last few months. I felt more relaxed and able to open up and engage in conversations.

Through my conversations with Dr. Gruenewald, I realized that I can become very impatient with people and that I have really high expectations of myself and others and hate to see them disappointed. I mentioned to him that I've often been perceived as arrogant and that I didn't think this was the case at all, but people often misunderstood me.

I just like to get things right and find it extremely annoying if people who should be knowledgeable in certain areas don't get their facts straight. I found teachers particularly annoying because they had an automatic claim to always being right and never admitted making mistakes. I couldn't stand their hypocritical behavior and the way they demanded respect despite not respecting me at all. I just couldn't understand how this didn't seem to matter to other people.

I felt, though, that I often got things a bit out of perspective, and I wanted to be more patient and slower to judge others. I didn't like the fact that I sometimes treated people, even friends, unfairly because of my quick temper.

I agreed to work on my relationship with the teacher after Dr. Gruenewald introduced the Preparing for a Challenging Conversation exercise to me. I was keen to try this exercise because I felt that this relationship had so much impact on my life at present and for the future and I hoped the exercise would help.

At times I had been extremely harsh in my judgments of myself and others. I understood that being kinder to myself and learning to accept my own weaknesses would help me become kinder toward others.

After two weeks of practicing the Transforming Challenging Relationships exercise, I felt that my attitude toward my teacher had changed. At times I was now able to see the teacher's point of view. I had still disagreements, but they seemed more constructive. Sometimes I could even convince my teacher of my own view of things or clarify

CASE STUDY: FRUSTRATION OF A TEENAGER

facts, like dates, that the teacher got wrong. I think that's because I wasn't so aggressive anymore.

Gradually I became more aware of my own actions and how they influence others. My temper has calmed down considerably and I also get along better with my family. The exercise taught me to be more compassionate and accepting of myself and others.

Imagining future events in a positive way was particularly helpful.

Reflecting compassionately on myself and others and mentally rehearsing future events now helps me deal with people I used to find hard to take. I'm also better with exam situations.

Recently I went to a few job interviews and felt that they went very well. Out of four interviews, I was offered three jobs. In the past, I usually found the interviews rather annoying and resented the interviewers' superior behavior. I think now that might have been because I have been putting on a rather arrogant act.

I feel more confident now because I'm able to rehearse the situations mentally and therefore can act more naturally in potentially stressful situations. I believe I've changed, and more people seem to like me. In the past, although I had good friends, I had problems with older people in authority.

I have now taken a year off after graduation to do some traveling and possibly some teaching in developing countries. It's pretty ironic that I'm even thinking about that.

Somehow, I've learned a lot about myself through the exercises and I'm more interested in other people. This makes me more understanding and patient. I'm planning to start college after my year off.

–Tom R., age 18

Summary and Conclusion

We started by examining the physiology of stress and resilience, including underlying body rhythms, heart rate variability, and autonomic nervous system balance. We found that it's important to establish and maintain good body rhythms for emotional and physical health and performance.

As we saw, this involves creating a physiology of engagement and flow in which sympathetic and parasympathetic activity are balanced and simultaneously active and strong.

Then we continued by looking at the psychology of resilience: negative emotions, positive feelings, and engagement.

Here we saw the importance of

- Recognizing and overcoming negative emotions and establishing positive feelings for good health and performance.
- Shifting from negative emotions to positive feelings, core elements of adaptive resilience.
- Engagement: "Burn on instead of burn out."

Possible obstacles to regeneration and recovery also figured here.

Subsequently, in the bulk of the book, we explored a range of exercises that can help you develop adaptive resilience. By regularly practicing these techniques, readers can learn how to harness pressures and transform stress and extreme emotions into health, happiness, and lasting peak performance. The techniques will help you

- Stay well during crises, challenges, and continual change.
- Improve health, performance, judgment, and decision-making.
- Enhance interactions with fellow human beings.

I believe everyone's life can be enhanced by these simple techniques as part of a routine. Taking the short time needed each day to put one or two of these exercises into action can have surprising benefits and lead to greater fulfillment in every realm of life. The ills we see everywhere in society today start with each individual, and that, too, is where we can start addressing them. The more we try to improve our own lives using these simple methods, the more our greater well-being will spread to others around us.

The practical tools and techniques and simple exercises in this book have been created to help you develop resilience, improve your well-being and health, and deal effectively with your stress. You've reached the end, and you should now know how to

- Understand how life's challenges affect your health, well-being, and performance.
- Deal with challenges and stress effectively.
- Improve relationships at work and at home.
- Deepen your inner leadership skills.
- Have more energy and balance throughout the day.
- Develop greater resilience and become less prone to burnout and extreme stress.
- Improve your health, well-being, and performance.

Your best future self is waiting for you. Are you ready to meet? Let's get started!

About the Author

DR. PETER GRUENEWALD, MD

is an internationally recognized expert in the field of adaptive resilience, stress, and performance.

Peter is an associate fellow at SAID Business School, Oxford University, and runs workshops in adaptive resilience for professionals, senior leaders, and managers in the private and public sectors.

Peter is the author of the book *The Quiet Heart: Putting Stress into Its Place*.[54]

He is a founder and managing director of Adaptive Resilience Ltd. He is also a cofounder and Chief Medical Officer of RCube Health, a digital health start-up company that has developed a mobile app for stress management and resilience (RCube).

Peter works as an Honorary Clinical Specialist in Sleep Medicine and General Medicine for the University College London Hospital (Royal Hospital for Integrated Medicine) and in private practice.

FREE DOWNLOAD

The breath pacer for your Coherence Exercise combines slow, deep pacing at 5.5 breathing cycles per minute with brainwave entrainment at gamma 40 Hz embedded in soundscapes and music. Using the breath pacer helps immerse you in the experience and lead you into a state of engagement and balance between focus and relaxation. It also enhances the beneficial physiological changes in breathing and heart, ANS, and brain activity. It's a potent training device that you should use for about six weeks, and then it may be beneficial to continue practicing the exercise without it.

Don't worry if you can't follow all the instructions instantly. With a little practice, you'll grow into this meditation and it will become second nature for you. Please use headphones when listening to the breath pacer.

You can download the MP3 files and choose from breath pacers in different soundscapes (music).

Caution: Do not listen to the audio file and do not practice the relaxation training while driving or operating machinery.

DOWNLAD NOW (Click here)
https://www.bestfutureself.org/breath-pacer-free-download

YouTube Resources
You can find a number of highly informative and entertaining third-party videos on my website.

VISIT NOW (Click here)
https://www.bestfutureself.org/youtube-resources

References

1. Angela Duckworth. TED Talk. Grit: The Power of passion and perseverance. https://www.ted.com/talks/angela_lee_duckworth_the_key_to_success_grit/transcript?language=en
2. Duckworth, Grit, London.
3. Mihaly Csíkszentmihályi, "Flow and the Foundations of Positive Psychology: The Collected Works of Mihaly Csikszentmihalyi. Springer, New York (8 Aug. 2014)
4. Mihaly Csíkszentmihályi, Flow: The Psychology of Happiness, New Ed. (Ebury Digital, 2013), London, Kindle.
5. Martin Seligman, The Hope Circuit: A Psychologist's Journey from Helplessness to Optimism (London: Nicholas Brealey, 2018).
6. Martin Seligman, Learned Optimism: How to Change Your Mind and Your Life (London: Nicholas Brealey, 2018).
7. Daniel Goleman, Emotional Intelligence. Why It Can Matter More Than IQ (London: Bloomsbury, 2009).
8. Martin Seligman, Flourish: A New Understanding of Happiness and Well-Being—and How to Achieve Them (London: Nicholas Brealey, 2011), Kindle.
9. Chrisanthy Vlachakis et al., "Human Emotions on the Onset of Cardiovascular and Small Vessel Related Diseases," In Vivo 32, no. 4 (July/August 2018): 859–70.
10. Ed Diener and Micaela Y. Chan. "Happy People Live Longer: Subjective Well-Being Contributes to Health and Longevity." Applied Psychology: Health and Well-Being 3, no. 1 (March 2011): 1–43, https://doi.org/10.1111/j.1758-0854.2010.01045.x.
11. American Psychological Association, "The Road to Resilience," apa.org, 2014, https://uncw.edu/studentaffairs/committees/pdc/documents/the%20road%20to%20resilience.pdf.

12 Diener and Chan, "Happy People."

13 Brian Chin et al., "Marital status as a predictor of diurnal salivary cortisol levels and slopes in a community sample of healthy adults," Psychoneuroendocrinology 78 (April 2017): 68–75, https://doi.org/10.1016/j.psyneuen.2017.01.016.

14 Jerry Suls and James Bunde, "Anger, Anxiety, and Depression as Risk Factors for Cardiovascular Disease: The Problems and Implications of Overlapping Affective Dispositions," Psychological Bulletin 131, no. 2 (March 2005): 260–300, https://doi.apa.org/doi/10.1037/0033-2909.131.2.260.

15 Csíkszentmihályi, Flow.

16 Michele M. Tugade and Barbara L. Fredrickson, "Resilient Individuals Use Positive Emotions to Bounce Back From Negative Emotional Experiences," Journal of Personality and Social Psychology 86, no. 2 (February 2004): 320–33, https://doi.apa.org/doi/10.1037/0022-3514.86.2.320.

17 Paul M. Lehrer and Richard Gevirtz, "Heart Rate Variability Biofeedback: How and Why Does It Work?" Frontiers in Psychology 5 (July 2014): 1–9, https://doi.org/10.3389/fpsyg.2014.00756.

18 Paul M. Lehrer et al., "Resonant Frequency Biofeedback Training to Increase Cardiac Variability: Rationale and Manual for Training," Applied Psychophysiology and Biofeedback 25, no. 3 (October 2000): 177–189, https://doi.org/10.1023/A:1009554825745.

19 Bradley M. Appelhans and Linda J. Luecken, "Heart Rate Variability as an Index of Regulated Emotional Responding," Review of General Psychology 10, no. 3 (September 2006): 229–40, https://doi.org/10.1037%2F1089-2680.10.3.229.

20 Raymond Trevor Bradley et al., "Emotion Self-Regulation, Psychophysiological Coherence, and Test Anxiety: Results from an Experiment Using Electrophysiological Measures," Applied Psychophysiology and Biofeedback 35, no. 4 (December 2010): 261–83, https://doi.org/10.1007/s10484-010-9134-x.

21 Maria Katsamanis Karavidas et al. "Preliminary Results of an Open Label Study of Heart Rate Variability Biofeedback for the Treatment of Major Depression," Applied Psychophysiology and Biofeedback 32, no. 1 (March 2007): 19–30, https://doi.org/10.1007/s10484-006-9029-z.

22 Auditya Purwandini Sutarto et al., "Resonant Breathing Biofeedback Training for Stress Reduction Among Manufacturing Operators," International Journal of Occupational Safety and Ergonomics 18, no. 4 (January 2012): 549–61, https://doi.org/10.1080/10803548.2012.11076959.

23 Gregg Henriques et al., "Exploring the Effectiveness of a Computer-Based Heart Rate Variability Biofeedback Program in Reducing Anxiety in College Students," Applied Psychophysiology and Biofeedback 36, no. 2 (June 2011): 101–12, https://doi.org/10.1007/s10484-011-9151-4.

24 Richard P. Brown et al., "Breathing Practices for Treatment of Psychiatric and Stress-Related Medical Conditions," Psychiatric Clinics of North America 36, no. 1 (March 2013): 121–140, https://doi.org/10.1016/j.psc.2013.01.001.

25 Rollin McCraty et al., "The Impact of a New Emotional Self-Management Program on Stress, Emotions, Heart Rate Variability, DHEA, and Cortisol," Integrative Physiological and Behavioral Sciences 33, no. 2 (April 1998): 151–70, https://doi.org/10.1007/bf02688660.

26 Mike J. Gross et al., "Abbreviated Resonant Frequency Training to Augment Heart Rate Variability and Enhance On-Demand Emotional Regulation in Elite Sport Support Staff," Applied Psychophysiology and Biofeedback 41, no. 3 (September 2016): 263–74, https://doi.org/10.1007/s10484-015-9330-9.

27 Auditya Purwandini Sutarto et al., "Heart Rate Variability (HRV) Biofeedback: A New Training Approach for Operator's Performance Enhancement," Journal of Industrial Engineering and Management 3, no. 1 (June 2010): 176–98, http://dx.doi.org/10.3926/jiem.2010.v3n1.p176-198.

28 Terri L. Zucker et al., "The Effects of Respiratory Sinus Arrhythmia Biofeedback on Heart Rate Variability and Posttraumatic Stress Disorder Symptoms: A Pilot Study," Applied Psychophysiology and Biofeedback 34, no. 2 (June 2009): 135–43, https://doi.org/10.1007/s10484-009-9085-2.

29 Kennon M. Sheldon and Sonja Lyubomirsky, "How to Increase and Sustain Positive Emotion: The Effects of Expressing Gratitude and Visualizing Best Possible Selves," Journal of Positive Psychology 1, no. 2 (2006): 73–82, https://doi.org/10.1080/17439760500510676.

30 Robert Emmons and Michael E. McCullough, "Counting Blessings Versus Burdens: An Experimental Investigation of Gratitude and Subjective Well-Being," Journal of Personality and Social Psychology 84, no. 2 (February 2003): 377–89, https://doi.apa.org/doi/10.1037/0022-3514.84.2.377.

31 Jeffrey J. Froh et al., "Counting Blessings in Early Adolescents: An Experimental Study of Gratitude and Subjective Well-Being," Journal of School Psychology 46, no. 2 (April 2008): 213–33, https://doi.org/10.1016/j.jsp.2007.03.005.

32 Jeffrey J. Froh et al., "Gratitude in Children and Adolescents: Development, Assessment, and School-Based Intervention (2007)," School Psychology Forum 2, no. 1 (Fall 2007).

33 For more about the benefits of exercising gratitude, see Kori D. Miller, "14 Health Benefits of Practicing Gratitude According to Science," positivepsychology.com, May 20, 2020, https://positivepsychology.com/benefits-of-gratitude/; Alice M. Isen et al., "The Influence of Positive Affect on Clinical Problem Solving," Medical Decision Making 11, no. 3 (July/September 1991): 221–7, https://doi.org/10.1177%2F0272989X9101100313; Alice M. Isen et al., "Positive Affect Facilitates Creative Problem Solving," Journal of Personality and Social Psychology 52, no. 6 (June 1987): 1122–31, https://doi.apa.org/doi/10.1037/0022-3514.52.6.1122; and F. Gregory Ashby et al., "A Neuropsychological Theory of Positive Affect and Its Influence on Cognition," Psychological Review 106, no. 3 (July 1999): 529–50, https://doi.apa.org/doi/10.1037/0033-295X.106.3.529.

34 Hildur Finnbogadóttir and Dorthe Berntsen, "Looking at Life from Different Angles: Observer Perspective during Remembering and Imagining Distinct Emotional Events," Psychology of Consciousness: Theory, Research, and Practice 1, no. 4 (2014): 387–406, https://doi.org/10.1037/CNS0000029.

35 See Melanie Gregg et al., "The Imagery Ability, Imagery Use, and Performance Relationship," The Sport Psychologist 19, no. 1 (2005): 93–99, https://pdfs.semanticscholar.org/cb93/ab4c2c70da9a0d52aedc5859640eda00978d.pdf; and David Eldred-Evans et al., "Using the Mind as a Simulator: A Randomized Controlled Trial of Mental Training," Journal of Surgical Education 70, no. 4 (July/August 2013): 544–51, https://doi.org/10.1016/j.jsurg.2013.04.003.

36 Shad Helmstetter: "What to say when you talk to yourself," Park Avenue Press (2011)

37 Mai-Chuan Wang et al., "Purpose in Life and Reasons for Living as Mediators of the Relationship between Stress, Coping, and Suicidal Behavior," Journal of Positive Psychology 2, no. 3 (June 2007): 195–204, https://doi.org/10.1080/17439760701228920.

38 Sven Asmus et al., "The Impact of Goal-Setting on Worker Performance—Empirical Evidence from a Real-Effort Production Experiment," Procedia CIRP 26, (2015): 127–32, https://doi.org/10.1016/j.procir.2015.02.086.

39 P. Christopher Earley et al., "Task Planning and Energy Expended: Exploration of How Goals Influence Performance," Journal of Applied Psychology 72, no. 1 (1987): 107–14, https://doi.apa.org/doi/10.1037/0021-9010.72.1.107.

40 On the effectiveness of self-talk, see Antonis Hatzigeorgiadis et al., "Mechanisms Underlying the Self-Talk–Performance Relationship: The Effects of Motivational Self-Talk on Self-Confidence and Anxiety,"

Psychology of Sport and Exercise 10, no. 1 (2009): 186–92, https://doi.org/10.1016/j.psychsport.2008.07.009; Chris P. Neck and Charles C. Manz, "Thought Self-Leadership: The Influence of Self-Talk and Mental Imagery on Performance," Journal of Organizational Behavior 13 (1992): 681–99, https://doi.org/10.1002/job.4030130705; and David Tod et al., "Effects of Self-Talk: A Systematic Review," Journal of Sport and Exercise Psychology 33, no. 5 (October 2011): 666–87, https://doi.org/10.1123/jsep.33.5.666.

41 Genevive R. Meredith et al. Minimum Time Dose in Nature to Positively Impact the Mental Health of College-Aged Students, and How to Measure It: A Scoping Review. Front. Psychol., 14 January 2020 https://doi.org/10.3389/fpsyg.2019.02942

42 Richard Louv, Last Child in the Woods: Saving Our Children from Nature-Deficit Disorder (London: Atlantic Books, 2013).

43 On the benefits of time in nature for mental health, see Mardie Townsend and Rona Weerasuriya, Beyond Blue to Green: The Benefits of Contact with Nature for Mental Health and Well-Being (Melbourne, Australia: Beyond Blue Limited, 2010); and Diana E. Bowler et al., "A Systematic Review of Evidence for the Added Benefits to Health of Exposure to Natural Environments," BMC Public Health 10 (August 2010): 456, https://doi.org/10.1186/1471-2458-10-456.

44 Rudolf Steiner. Goethean Science (Liverpool: Mercury Press, 1988).

45 Shinya Kubota et al., "A Study of the Effects of Active Listening on Listening Attitudes of Middle Managers," Journal of Occupational Health 46, no. 1 (February 2004): 60–7, https://doi.org/10.1539/joh.46.60.

46 Lynn Kacperck, "Non-Verbal Communication: The Importance of Listening," British Journal of Nursing 6, no. 5 (December 2014): 27, https://doi.org/10.12968/bjon.1997.6.5.275.

47 Nancy Kline, Time to Think: Listening to Ignite the Human Mind (London: Cassell, 2002). The power of effective listening is recognized as the essential tool of good management.

48 Carl Rogers, Client Centred Therapy: Its Current Practice, Implications and Theory (London: Robinson, 2003).

49 Sachiko Mineyama et al., "Supervisors' Attitudes and Skills for Active Listening with Regard to Working Conditions and Psychological Stress Reactions among Subordinate Workers," Journal of Occupational Health 49 (2007) 1. https://doi.org/10.1539/joh.49.81.

50 Otto Scharmer and Katrin Kaufer, Leading from the Emerging Future: From Ego-System to Eco-System Economies (Oakland, CA: Berrett-Koehler, 2013).

51 Carl R. Rogers, On Becoming a Person: A Therapist's View of Psychotherapy, 2nd ed. (Boston, Massachusetts: Houghton Mifflin, 1995); Rogers, Client Centred Therapy; Carl R. Rogers and Barry Stevens, Person to Person: The Problem of Being Human (Lafayette, CA: Real People Press, 1967); Carl R. Rogers et al., On Becoming an Effective Teacher—Person-Centered Teaching, Psychology, Philosophy, and Dialogues with Carl R. Rogers and Harold Lyon (London: Routledge, 2013).

52 Jeanne C. Watson, "Re-Visioning Empathy," in Humanistic Psychotherapies: Handbook of Research and Practice, eds. David J. Cain and Julius Seeman (Washington, DC: American Psychological Association, 2002), 445–71.

53 Graham L. Bradley and Amanda C. Campbell, "Managing Difficult Workplace Conversations: Goals, Strategies, and Outcomes," International Journal of Business Communication 53, no. 4 (October 2016): 443–64.

54 Peter Gruenewald, The Quiet Heart: Putting Stress in Its Place (Edinburgh: Floris Books, 2007).

Printed in Great Britain
by Amazon